The End is Here

by
Homer Slack

The End Is Here

Copyright © 2012 Homer A. Slack

Second Edition: December 2018

All rights reserved. No part of this publication can be reproduced or transmitted in any form or by any means without permission in writing from Author.

Verses are mainly quoted from two versions of the bible, the NIV and the NKJV.

Holy Bible, New International Version®, NIV® Copyright ©1973, 1978, 1984, 2011 by Biblica, Inc.® Used by permission. All rights reserved worldwide.

The New King James Version®. Copyright © 1982 by Thomas Nelson. Used by permission. All rights reserved.

Published by Select Arrow
www.selectArrow.net

ISBN: 9781791552596

Cover design and interior layout: Homer Slack
Editor: Angela Slack

Printed by CreateSpace

ACKNOWLEDGEMENTS

I must say a very big thank you firstly to God who by His rich mercies and grace has poured into me that I may pour out to you. I would also like to thank my wife Angela for her support during the tough times when we made sacrifices by foregoing things we would love to have and do to see to it that quality time was spent to produce quality material with God's help. Thanks also to my children Dorian and Briana and my brothers and sisters in Christ, Sharon and John Bett, Janet Clark, Denise White, Lynda and Michael Smith who have given me immense encouragement and support. Thank you all very much.

Table of Contents

Chapter   **Page**

1. The End According to Joel 1
2. Before the Great and Terrible Day 7
3. Escaping the Day of God's Wrath 15
4. The Day of the Lord 23
5. Armageddon God and Man at War 29
6. The Great Falling Away 37
7. The Great Tribulation 59
8. The Great Deception 65
9. Earth's Desolation 73
10. Heed the Warning 79

Preface

At the time of the first edition of this book, in the year 2012, there were many unusual predictions or reminders that time could possibly be ending that very year. Among them the ancient Mayan calendar which ended December of that year was suggested by many to be a sign that time will not have continued beyond then. It was the 100 year anniversary of the sinking of the Titanic, reminding us that the best of our technologies and systems, though thought indestructible, can crash suddenly and sink us without warning and by the least of the forces of nature.

There are some issues concerning scriptures and the plan of God that ought to be settled in our minds by now. One such issue is the question of when are the end times, a question that has been answered in a number of places throughout scriptures. We are presently living in the end times and have been doing so for over 2000 years now.

The imminence of Christ's return was so alive in the spirits of the apostles that their writing seems to suggest that they were expecting that it could happen in their lifetime. The issues we will look at therefore, will not be with an aim to answer 'if we are in the end times' but for us to wonder at what point in the end times we are. We will mainly look at end time events as they were given to us by Jesus, the prophet Joel and others.

We will begin by looking at the prophet Joel's visions and warnings which could be described as the preaching of the gospel as it very closely resembles the message preached by John the Baptist, Jesus and the New Testament apostles. We will also look at Jesus' outline of end time events recorded mainly in Matthew 24. You may want to read these chapters through in one go to understand them in context.

If you are a bit sleepy spiritually this book should help to wake you up or if you know anyone who is in a state of spiritual slumber please see to it that they get a copy. *"Awake Oh sleeper, arise from the dead, and Christ shall give you light."* Ephesians 5:14

Chapter 1

Part 1: It is Coming

The End According to Joel

Joel received a message from God by way of a vision. His vision outlined the events of the end that were very frightening and sobering. It all pointed to a day referred to as the 'Day of The Lord'. The core message is a call to action for all those who are to escape the perils of this day. There is a stark warning to those who will not respond. The day of the Lord will be the most terrifying day of destruction and calamities ever known to mankind. We need a clear understanding of what is coming and what we need to do to escape it.

One year's measure of rain fell in three days in Jamaica. This happened back in the early eighties but I will never forget it. A man heading home in his big truck came to a bridge that he's travelled for many years. It was night and there was no street lamps so he battled the poor visibility depending only on his vehicle's headlights. This bridge was part of a major roadway linking two towns so it was sturdily built and heavily travelled.

There was water flowing everywhere, across roadways and down hillsides so as he approached the bridge it came as no surprise that he was seeing a lot of water. What he didn't realise however, was that the rushing water had taken the bridge. He was just about leaving the tarmac to begin what used to be the bridge when he realised there was no bridge there. He found out just in time to stop his heavy vehicle, jump out and run toward firmer ground as he watched the swelling river pull his truck in and carry it away.

As he stood in the roadway, wet, frantic and frightened he noticed a pair of headlights heading towards him. As it got closer he noticed it was a medium sized passenger vehicle. It was coming at full speed so he made every effort to stand where he could be seen and began to wave frantically for the driver to stop. As the vehicle went by him he realised it was a minibus filled with people who took no notice of his desperate shouting and frantic waving. Could they all have been thinking how inconsiderate he was to be hoping to board the bus soaked and dripping? How could they misunderstand his desperate motioning and panic filled shouting? Was there not even an iota of concern for his well being in such a torrential downpour? Their indifference cost them their lives. He watched as they all plunged full speed to their deaths into the swelling, rushing river.

How misunderstood and marginalised today are the preachers who shout, "turn back, turn back, repent, repent!" They are snared at, put down, pushed out and blocked more by so called 'Christian leaders' than anyone else. The popular gospel today is spoken softly and is void of rebuke or warning because the typical believer cannot handle the trumpeting volume of the warning preacher. Nothing has changed really for so also they treated the prophets of old. The lucky ones were cast into dungeons while others were killed. It is believed Isaiah was shoved down a hollow log before sawn in two.

Joel has been to the end in his vision, he has seen it. Now he is waving and shouting frantically to us. Will we take heed and act or will we misunderstand him and take offence?

The Man Who Foresaw The End
> Because nothing is known of Joel beyond what the opening verse of his book states, he has been styled "The Anonymous Prophet." Scripture is silent as to his birthplace, parentage and rank. All we know is that he was a son of Pethuel, or Bethuel as the LXX expresses it. But who Pethuel is no one knows. Its meaning, however, is significant, "vision of God," and springs from a word implying "to open the eyes."
>
> Joel was a common name among the Hebrews and is still so among the Orientals. The use of his name as "the son of Pethuel" was necessary to distinguish him from the other Joels. It would seem as if his home was in Jerusalem or its immediate neighborhood. Thus he speaks repeatedly of Zion, the children of Zion, Judah and Jerusalem, the children of Judah and Jerusalem.
>
> It may be that Joel was a Jew of Jerusalem, and owing to his peculiar mention of priests, a priest-prophet himself (Joel 1:9, 10). His references to the Temple and its worship are frequent. It is also likely that he lived and prophesied in the early days of Joash and Jehoida, 870-865 b.c., while the victory of Jehoshaphat was fresh in the nation's memory. For this reason he is termed "The Pioneer Prophet."
> All the Men of the Bible/All the Women of the Bible Compilation - Zondervan - Copyright 2005 By Herbert Lockyer

Joel is possibly the best known of the minor prophets because he was the one that clearly prophesied the outpouring of the Holy Spirit that was fulfilled on the Day of Pentecost as recorded in Acts chapter two. Joel was further legitimised when Peter, one of Jesus' inner circle disciples, stood up and quoted his prophecy that was fulfilled to the letter. His authenticity is beyond question and therefore nothing that he prophesies must be taken for granted. They will all likewise be fulfilled.

The book of Joel outlines the prophecies given to him as he is used by God to forewarn of the impending judgment. This judgment comes as God's response to man's blatant disregard, rebellion and blasphemy against His laws that were given to keep mankind and nature in perfect harmony with their Creator.

The apocalyptic themes in Joel are confirmed by other prophets who were likewise gripped by visions of futuristic events but had to describe them within the limitations of their current reality. Studying Joel today, in our time, could possibly clarify some of what the prophet was struggling to describe as our present reality may possibly interpret these predicted events within the context of technological advancements like atomic weapons. In our present context we see even nature itself giving signs of pending global meltdown due to our destructive lifestyle and misuse of technology on the planet.

As we advance through Joel we will come to realise that the apocalyptic theme will be interrupted at times with messages of blessings. Don't let this confuse you, his account is not given in chronological order. Unlike some other prophets, Joel's prophecy is all about the end times. His account however, starts at the end of the end times then goes back to the beginning before again returning to the end.

These prophets received God's word through visions, dreams and impressions of the Holy Spirit but such prophecies tend not to be as clear as crystal. A picture is painted, it seems, using a mixture of places, people, times and circumstances. Our dreams also sometimes blend places and people from different time lines and experiences.

Joel's prophecy is no less of a puzzle as it clearly crisscrosses the time line of the end using a blend of soldiers and insects, natural armies as well as supernatural ones. We will at times ask ourselves, "Is he addressing natural Israel only or all of God's people throughout the world, or could the same prophecy be applied to both?" Understanding the specific times and events of Joel's prophecy could be quite a challenge but not so with its message. The message in his vision is as clear as crystal.

This work therefore, will not attempt to answer all the questions and solve all the mysteries but will focus on its obvious message, especially proving that this message forms a thread that runs throughout all scripture.

Chapter 2

Before the Great and Terrible Day

Based on Joel Chapter 1 to 2:12

The beginning of Joel's prophecy did not hesitate to throw us into the action. Like an action packed movie that opens right in the middle of the battle, Joel's prophecy starts with a cry for people to pay attention and listen to what he has seen. What he has seen is not good. He sees devastation and unrivalled destruction. The rhetorical question is asked,

Joel 1:2
"Has anything like this ever happened in your days or in the days of your forefathers?" The answer clearly is, no!

The prophecy should never be forgotten, dismissed or diminished in any way but must be passed down from one generation to another. Each generation (ours could be the final one) is closer to this apocalypse that will make past tragedies and wars look like child's play.

The information at times seems sketchy but this is what he saw.

Joel 1:4-7
"What the locust swarm has left the great locusts have eaten; what the great locusts have left the young locusts have eaten; what the young locusts have left other locusts have eaten... A nation has invaded my land, powerful and without number; it has the teeth of a lion, the fangs of a lioness. It has laid waste my vines ruined my fig trees. It has stripped off their bark and thrown it away, leaving their branches white."

No one knows exactly what it all means and I would not dare to try and say conclusively. Here therefore, is one of the many possibilities. In chapter one the sketches in his vision seems to suggest that destruction will be coming in waves. First the swarms, then the great locust, then the young locust and finally other random locusts. If the locust symbolises human armies as verse six seems to indicate, the first wave, the swarm, could be speaking of a powerful nation invading God's land Israel. Like locust, the army of this nation is beyond numbering and like locusts they will cause unimaginable devastation. They are a strong force that will overwhelm, grip and rip through the Jewish nation with the force of a lioness tearing through her prey. We will see later that an attack on Israel by forces that will surround Jerusalem is also predicted by Jesus.

Usually we try to encourage people so that their grieving would not be prolonged. In this case however, Joel is encouraging his people to grieve. He interjected three times over eight verses to remind us to weep, wail, mourn, grieve etc. Joel is seeing dark days ahead. Verse twelve of chapter one drives home the point. *"Surely the joy of mankind is withered away."*

He mentioned the joy of mankind not just of Israel. Could this be an indication that what began with one nation attacking Israel will escalate beyond her boundaries. Maybe others of her enemies will try to take advantage of the opportunity while she is weakened, hence the second wave, the great locust? Could it be that the first nation's strength was in numbers but joining them later were the more powerful among Israel's enemies. Soon another wave would come from other smaller and less experienced opportunistic nations. The final wave may just be small bands of Jewish haters seeking to take advantage of the the large scale attack on Israel. All this time no allied nation came to Israel's rescue. Their excuse maybe that they have their hands full or maybe at that time Israel will have no allies. Remember this would be happening in the later parts of the last days. There are wars and rumours of wars everywhere and Israel's best allies, if any, may be weakened and overstretched.

So What's Happening?
The first possibility:
The army that invades Israel uses biological weapons that target vegetation destroying crops and stripping trees.

Joel 1:10
"The fields are ruined, the ground is dried up; the grain is destroyed…"

When all is parched, withered and dry, fires begin to burn out of control. Joel speaks of fires and food shortage which no doubt will result in famine etc. as Jesus himself also predicted. Joel continues…

Joel 1:19-20
"To you, Lord, I call, for fire has devoured the pastures in the wilderness and flames have burned up all the trees of the field. Even the wild animals pant for you; the streams of water have dried up and fire has devoured the pastures in the wilderness."

Second possibility:
The trees and fields could be just metaphors used to represent people and groups of people like towns and cities. We see Jesus using such metaphors several times in His parables. Again, drought, famine and fires etc. may be used as an indication that there will be great hardships, struggle and persecution. *"...when these things begin to happen, look up and lift up your heads, because your redemption draws near."* Luke 21:28

Third possibility:
The third possibility is that both are true. An attack upon Israel is just a natural manifestation of a spiritual reality where God's people everywhere will be coming under serious spiritual attack. The physical droughts and famines could possibly be paralleled by a Spiritual drought and famine.

Joel knows that these are signs of the end. *"Alas for that day! For the day of the Lord is near..."* Joel 1:15 The day of the Lord is not yet but it's close and these are only events leading up to it. Man is used to bring the great destruction seen so far, The day of the Lord however, will see destruction brought by God's heavenly hosts. It will be totally mind blowing. Wars among nations will be an early indication. The war against Israel and God's elect will tell us we are at the very door but all this will culminate in the 'day of the Lord.'

Joel Chapter 2:1-12 - The Day of the Lord Is Near
This Day is no secret but is well documented throughout Scripture both in the Old and New Testaments.

Joel 2:1-2
"For the day of the Lord is coming, for it is at hand: A day of darkness and gloominess, A day of clouds and thick darkness..."

It is the day Jesus returns and God pours out His wrath upon evil mankind. Much of Joel's prophecy is taken up with the events of this day and the events leading up to this day (we will examine this in chapter four of this book). Joel also pleads with his people to make every effort to be found in right standing with God before these things begin to happen. We too should be pleading with our generation and with even more urgency.

It is here in chapter two of Joel that we discover another army, referred to as God's army. This army was more in numbers and had greater destructive capabilities than anything ever seen before or will ever be seen on earth again. The end will be marked by two history making events, 1. man at his most destructive, the great tribulation 2. the day of God's wrath, the great desolation. God is behind both events. As the picture of what is to come unveils it becomes obvious that one cannot over emphasise the need to cry out to God for mercy. First the earthly host rising up against God's people then comes the heavenly host when God will rain down never seen before destruction upon the earth. If you are reading this, remember that we are presently living within the time line of Joel's prophecy.

Joel 2:2
"Like dawn spreading across the mountains a large and mighty army comes, such as never was of old nor ever will be in ages to come."

Joel starts chapter two with a frantic effort to get the people's attention. *"Blow the trumpet in Zion; sound the alarm on my holy hill."* Joel 2:1 Like a siren that sounds to warn a city that enemy bombers are approaching. Let the watchmen get up high and empty their lungs into that trumpet, let everyone hear the warning and know that an army like never seen before is on its way. Be afraid and tremble because the day of the Lord is near.

Listen to what he says in **Joel 2:3b - 10.** *"Before them the land is like the garden of Eden, behind them, a desert waste nothing escapes them... At the sight of them, nations are in anguish; every face turns pale... Before them the earth shakes, the sky trembles, the sun and moon are darkened, and the stars no longer shine."*

Other passages of scripture speaks of this army that will accompany our Lord on His return. Here is one, *"...when the Lord Jesus is revealed from heaven with His mighty angels, in flaming fire taking vengeance on those who do not know God, and on those who do not obey the gospel of our Lord Jesus Christ."* 2 Thessalonians 1:7-8 The vibration that resulted from the marching army will shake heaven and earth.

Almost all the accounts of the day of the Lord mentions the darkening of the sun and moon. We will speak more about this in a later chapter. What is important is that we know what to do to endure the wrath of wicked men and escape the wrath of an angry God.

Joel 2:11b
"The day of the LORD is great; it is dreadful. Who can endure it?"

Our Lord speaking through Joel tells us who will escape. Towards the end of a long chapter at verse 32 He refers to them as 'those who call on the name of the Lord.' It is this group, the callers on the Lord that will be saved from it.

John made this clear when he said to the religious leaders coming to be baptised, *"Brood of vipers! Who warned you to flee from the wrath to come?"* Matthew 3:7 John's message was exactly as Joel's and thank God some were taking his advice to repent and make things right with God so that they may not be swallowed up by what is approaching on the horizon. Listen to the Lord's advice through Joel...

Joel 2:12

"Now, therefore,' says the Lord, 'turn to Me with all your heart, with fasting, with weeping, and with mourning."

Peter also understood this. When asked on the Day of Pentecost by those who enquired about salvation he told them, *"Be saved from this perverse generation."* Acts 2:40 Why should people turn from this perverse generation repent and therein save themselves? Because God is about to destroy it, as He did Sodom. Turn to God that you may be 'raptured' before the day of God's wrath. Yes, raptured.

Many agree with me that believers will be taken out of the world before this great and terrible day. I believe we will, most naturally, be here for the great tribulation (I will speak more about this later) but not for the desolation that will take place on the day of the Lord. There are many scriptures in support of this but a good one is Luke's account of what Jesus said in Matthew 24:38. Here Jesus drew a comparison between what will happen in the end with what happened in the days of Noah. In the days of Noah when the floods were destroying all the inhabitants of the earth Noah and his family were kept safe in the ark by God who himself shut the door.

God did a similar thing during the plagues of Egypt by providing a place called Goshen for His people. The plagues did not affect Goshen where God's people were. During this same time the angel of death destroyed the first born of every household but did not touch those families that had the blood of the lamb over their doorposts or lintels.

So, according to Luke 17:27 disaster came only after Noah and his family were safely in the ark. And again, according to Luke 17:29, fire did not rain down upon Sodom until the day Lot and his family left safely.

Conclusion

Scripture clearly indicates that destruction, greater than we have ever known, is going to visit humanity from the hands of God and this time only those who are securely in Christ will be saved. As happened in the days of Lot and Noah destruction will come only after God's people are safely taken out.

"At that time his voice shook the earth, but now he has promised, 'Once more I will shake not only the earth but also the heavens.' The words 'once more' indicate the removing of what can be shaken—that is, created things—so that what cannot be shaken may remain. Therefore, since we are receiving a kingdom that cannot be shaken, let us be thankful, and so worship God acceptably with reverence and awe, for our "God is a consuming fire." Hebrews 12:26-29

God here is said to be a consuming fire. To escape His burning wrath we must repent, submit to His Lordship and worship Him with reverence and awe. It is a bad idea to lose our reverence for and our fear of God especially as the day of the Lord approaches. God is awesome but we are nothing, He doesn't need us but we desperately need Him. Accepting Jesus as God's sacrifice for our sins and serving Him acceptably with respect and reverence will save us on the day of His wrath. And that day is close.

Luke's report on Jesus' warning is very important. *"Be careful, or your hearts will be weighed down with carousing, drunkenness and the anxieties of life, and that day will close on you suddenly like a trap. For it will come on all those who live on the face of the whole earth. Be always on the watch, and pray that you may be able to escape all that is about to happen, and that you may be able to stand before the Son of Man."* Luke 21:34-36

Chapter 3

Escaping the Day of God's Wrath
A Call to Repentance

Based on Joel Chapter 2:12-28
True repentance
To discover the way of escape let us continue in Joel Chapter 2. Here we find proof that God cannot be criticised as one who is unjust or unbalanced in His judgement. Even at this point after many warnings and calls for repentance, yet again, God leaves us a way of escape. Yes judgement is at the door but remember even at this point salvation is available; through the complete work of Jesus Christ who shed His blood to satisfy the penalty for sin i.e. death. His resurrection signaled His triumph.

God speaks compassionately to His people through Joel's prophecy. He calls us back to that point when we understood and respected His awesome power. He pleads with us to bow our hearts and knees before Him. God's continuous and patient warning is a demonstration of His love. He could just warn us once and then send judgement, but He doesn't.

Joel 2:12-13
"Even now, declares the LORD, return to me with all your heart, with fasting and weeping and mourning. Rend your heart and not your garments." A superficial repentance will not work. Back then people in mourning would tear/rend their garment and cover themselves with ashes. The problem however, was that for many it was nothing more than a ritual. They went through the motions but had no true feeling of grief or regret. God through Joel was calling for a heartfelt repentance and not just a shallow show of religious penance.

Most of us will never have the status, the money or influence enough to bring us before earthly monarchs, but here the King of heaven and earth gives an open invitation for all to come to Him, the only place where there will be safety on that day. The requirement is nothing more than a broken heart and a contrite spirit where fasting, weeping and mourning is an outward sign of our inner brokenness.

> "Until a man has gotten into trouble with his heart he is not likely to get out of trouble with God." The Root of the Righteous by A. W. Tozer, Pg 39

As New Testament saints we know now that this call to repentance was first given to Israel but is now, through the grace of Jesus Christ, extended to the rest of the Gentile world. We who were destined for God's wrath have also been given a chance of escape through Jesus Christ. Repent and join those of us who will escape the terrors of the day of the Lord.

Repentance Defined

The dictionary meaning of repentance is to: "Feel or express sincere regret or remorse about one's wrongdoing or sin." (Oxford Dictionary) This meaning speaks only of a feeling but the biblical meaning of repentance goes a bit further and involves action. We must make a complete round about turn away from sin and towards Christ. Remember, Joel's prophecy is a call to action.

Note: If one only feels sorry but does not turn and head towards God, they have not repented.

Repentance is God's gift of recognition, it starts with the opening of our eyes so we can comprehend the reality of what is about to come upon the earth. For us living in this generation more than any other, we will also see that Jesus loves us, that He is Lord and He alone can save us. Our disobedience and apathy towards God is turned to a love and appreciation of Jesus our Lord and saviour so we run to Him instead of away from Him.

Repentance is a must, it is essential for salvation. The person who does not repent will perish in unquenchable fire (read Luke 3:1-20 & Luke 13). Like Joel, the main theme of Jesus' and John the Baptist's message was repentance. Read Matthew 3:1 and Matthew 4:17. The disciples also preached repentance. Read Mark 6:12.

If you are reading this, it is not too late, the day of God's salvation has not yet come to an end. *"Behold, now is the accepted time; behold, now is the day of salvation."* 2 Corinthians 6:2 The day known as the day of salvation must first end for the day of God's wrath to start. As you read, no doubt it is late in the day but thank God the day of salvation has not yet closed. God will pardon our sins and cause us to escape His judgement if we call on Him. Hurry to the place of repentance, be quick about it, let us bow our knees and hearts because He who is the consuming fire is also quick to pardon and forgive. Yes, He is like that, it is His nature; He finds pleasure in blessing us not in destroying us. *"As you know, we consider blessed those who have persevered. You have heard of Job's perseverance and have seen what the Lord finally brought about. The Lord is full of compassion and mercy."* James 5:11

Blast the trumpet you preachers of the gospel, sound the call to gather the assembly. Something of grave importance is to be announced. We need a time of fasting and repentance, the pending terrors are not to be taken lightly.

> "When a nation calls its prime men to battle, homes are broken, weeping sweethearts say their goodbyes, businesses are closed, college careers are wrecked, factories are refitted for wartime production, rationing and discomforts are accepted – all for war. Can we do less for the greatest fight that this world has ever known outside of the cross- this end-time siege on sanity, morality and spirituality?"
> Revival God's Way by Leonard Ravenhill pg. 127

In Joel 2:16 the importance of the matter is emphasised. The call is to every person, adult or child, even the babe nursing at the breast. Wedding plans must be put on hold and honeymoons cut short. Let there be a meeting of the officials, let repentance take place at every level, every age group and every strata of society.

Joel continues with clear instructions, explaining not only who should repent but how it should be done and the words that should be used.

Joel 2:17
"Let the priests, who minister before the LORD, weep between the temple porch and the altar. Let them say, 'Spare your people, O LORD. Do not make your inheritance an object of scorn, a byword among the nations. Why should they say among the peoples, 'Where is their God?'" This prayer is significant because it shows that God's own people are at risk of coming under His wrath. If we love the world and live like them we will reap the same reward they will reap. God forbid that this should

happen to those who are called by His name. *"For God did not appoint us to suffer wrath but to receive salvation through our Lord Jesus Christ."* 1 Thessalonians 5:9

It is also significant because a promise and a covenant are at stake. We are asking God to show that He is a God who keeps His promises to save those who call upon Him and to further incorporate us into His family. The Psalmist knows about this, he says. *"For great is his love toward us, and the faithfulness of the LORD endures forever..."* Psalm 117:2

Salvation Instead of Condemnation

If we follow the instructions in Joel chapter 2 to repent we will get a positive response from God. He will respond with words of comfort and acts of blessings. The call to mourn and weep will change to reassurance and words of comfort telling us to not be afraid but to be glad and rejoice. This relief and reassurance affects everything around us, our families, friends and even our animals.

The promises to those who repent are in great contrast to the warnings for those who do not. The following describes a spiritual refreshing for those who heed the call to repent. As mentioned in our discussion of chapter one of Joel, though described in physical terms, the change spoken of here is figurative and have more to do with our spiritual reality than the physical one.

Joel 2:21-24

"Fear not, O land; be glad and rejoice, for the Lord has done marvelous things! Do not be afraid, you beasts of the field; for the open pastures are springing up, and the tree bears its fruit; the fig tree and the vine yield their strength. Be glad then, you children of Zion, and rejoice in the Lord your God; for He has given you the former rain faithfully, and He will

cause the rain to come down for you— the former rain, and the latter rain in the first month. The threshing floors shall be full of wheat, and the vats shall overflow with new wine and oil."

In other words, God will refresh and restore our souls. Peter agrees on a spiritual interpretation and says, *"Repent, then, and turn to God, so that your sins may be wiped out, that times of refreshing may come from the Lord..."* Acts 3:19 We will have plenty to eat of the bread of life and plenty to drink of His life giving Spirit. Those who drink of the water that Jesus will give them shall never thirst (John 4:14). Well fed, refreshed and full of praise for the name of the LORD our God. When seen in this light it is clear that this utterance is a prophecy concerning salvation through Jesus Christ and the refreshing and renewing that follows.

A further detailed utterance concerning this 'latter rain' and 'new wine and oil' was what won Joel his fame. He continues...

Joel 2:28
"And it shall come to pass afterward that I will pour out My Spirit on all flesh..."

After what? After the coming of salvation. Those who could see through the eyes of the Spirit would have known from this prophetic utterance that Jesus' salvation would come before the promised outpouring of the Spirit. God's refreshing from on high includes His salvation and His Holy Spirit. Salvation has already come and the Holy Spirit has already been poured out so, for us today, God has already given the spring of living waters in the midst of this dry and parched land for all who will repent to partake and drink, bathe or even swim if you wish, in the glory and Spirit of God.

Conclusion

Let us be clear on this, let there be no misunderstanding here, nothing can stop the coming judgement. This judgement must come as a just and proper punishment for mankind's sin/rebellion against a Holy God. The soul who sins shall die (Ezekiel 18:20), that is, be suddenly separated from God's presence, fellowship and favour and be plunged into utter darkness and torment. Those who repent will be saved from a dark existence and become partakers of the great heavenly riches judgement will still come on the rebellious. The Lord will freely pardon, He does not hold grudges but we must first repent and Joel chapter 2b clearly reflects this. Isaiah also proclaimed, *"Let the wicked forsake his way and the evil man his thoughts. Let him turn to the LORD, and he will have mercy on him, and to our God, for he will freely pardon."* Isaiah 55:7

Repent therefore, and be saved from His wrath.

Chapter 4

The Day of the Lord

Based on Joel Chapter 2:30-32
The Day of the Lord
So what is this 'day of the Lord' we see referred to in both chapters one and two of Joel? This day is so frightening that heaven and earth will run away in fright and terror. It is the day when Jesus returns to the earth, the day God will judge the earth and destroy it because of the many sins that are committed here. The day God will consume the earth with fire and leave it bare and desolate. It is the day of God's wrath.

As mentioned earlier, there are signs that will indicate the imminence of that day and there are also horrifying events that will take place on the actual day. Nature will give us signs as this day draws nearer but the decay of human morals and character will be the surest sign.

We already observed a sudden shift in Joel's vision, the scene had changed and the whole stage was rearranged. He went from horrifying scenes of what would happen just before and on the day of the Lord to scenes of great blessings that would envelope those who heeded the call to repent before this day arrives. The scene is about to change again.

The invasion of Israel is but one of the many things that will happen leading up to the coming of this dreadful day. We have already experienced the coming of His salvation (this was fulfilled in Jesus) and the pouring out of His Spirit (that took place on the day of Pentecost), both promised for the end times according to Scriptures. These two significant events especially, was sent by God as a way of escape. The events that will signal the final curtain call are clearly given. A few are mentioned by Joel.

Joel 2:30-31
"I will show wonders in the heavens and on the earth, blood and fire and billows of smoke. The sun will be turned to darkness and the moon to blood before the coming of the great and dreadful day of the LORD."

Jesus said, *"Now when these things begin to happen, look up and lift up your heads, because your redemption draws near."* Luke 21:28 The end of the closing scene will return to terrifying displays. It will be loaded with horrifying spectaculars and finally the turning off of the heavenly lights.

In Matthew chapter 24, Jesus' disciples asked for clear signs that would indicate the end of time and based on Jesus' explanation backed by other prophecies we do have clarity on several things that will happen in the final few days at the closing of time. The most mentioned of them all however, is the fact that within the final few days or hours strange things will happen to celestial elements including the darkening of the sun, the moon and the stars. There is also quite a lot mentioned about planet wide fires and burning, much of which is caused by falling heavenly bodies, what we know today to be meteorites and asteroids (fire and brimstone). What happened to Sodom was a foreshadowing of what will happen to the whole world at the end.

A Day of Fires
Genesis 19:24 *"Then the Lord rained brimstone and fire on Sodom and Gomorrah, from the Lord out of the heavens."*

Jude confirms that what happened to wicked Sodom and Gomorrah will happen to all the world that will become just as sinful and wicked.

Jude 1:7 *"...as Sodom and Gomorrah, and the cities around them in a similar manner to these, having given themselves over to sexual immorality and gone after strange flesh, are set forth as an example, suffering the vengeance of eternal fire."*

Remember Joel spoke about these fires.
Joel 1:15-19 *"Alas for the day! For the day of the Lord is at hand; It shall come as destruction from the Almighty... O Lord, to You I cry out; For fire has devoured the open pastures, and a flame has burned all the trees of the field."*

Others spoke of these fires and failing/falling heavenly bodies.
2 Peter 3:7-10 *"By the same word the present heavens and earth are reserved for fire, being kept for the day of judgment and destruction of ungodly men. But do not forget this one thing, dear friends: With the Lord a day is like a thousand years, and a thousand years are like a day. The Lord is not slow in keeping his promise, as some understand slowness. He is patient with you, not wanting anyone to perish, but everyone to come to repentance. But the day of the Lord will come like a thief. The heavens will disappear with a roar; the elements will be **destroyed by fire**, and the earth and everything in it will be laid bare."* (Some manuscripts say 'be burned up')

2 Thessalonians 1:6-9 *"God is just: He will pay back trouble to those who trouble you and give relief to you who are troubled, and to us as well.*

*This will happen when the Lord Jesus is revealed from heaven **in blazing fire** with his powerful angels. He will punish those who do not know God and do not obey the gospel of our Lord Jesus. They will be punished with everlasting destruction and shut out from the presence of the Lord and from the majesty of his power..."*

Matthew 13:40-43 *"As the weeds are pulled up and **burned in the fire**, so it will be at the end of the age. The Son of Man will send out his angels, and they will weed out of his kingdom everything that causes sin and all who do evil. They will throw them into **the fiery furnace**, where there will be weeping and gnashing of teeth. Then the righteous will shine like the sun in the kingdom of their Father. He who has ears, let him hear."*

A Day of Falling/Failing Heavenly Bodies

Joel continues to describe what will happen in the time running up to the end or the day of the Lord.

Joel 2:10, 30-31 *"The earth quakes before them, the heavens tremble; **the sun and moon grow dark, and the stars diminish their brightness...** And I will show wonders in the heavens and in the earth: Blood and fire and pillars of smoke. **The sun shall be turned into darkness, and the moon into blood,** before the coming of the great and awesome day of the Lord."*

Joel 3:14-15 *"Multitudes, multitudes in the valley of decision! For the day of the Lord is near in the valley of decision. **The sun and moon will grow dark, and the stars will diminish their brightness."***

Isaiah 13:6-11 *"Wail, for the day of the Lord is at hand! It will come as destruction from the Almighty. Therefore all hands will be limp, every man's heart will melt, and they will be afraid. Pangs and sorrows will take hold of them; they will be in pain as a woman in childbirth; they* *will be amazed at one another; their faces will be like flames. Behold, the day of the Lord comes, cruel, with both wrath and fierce anger, to lay the land desolate; and He will destroy its sinners from it.* **For the stars of heaven and their constellations will not give their light; the sun will be darkened in its going forth, and the moon will not cause its light to shine.** *'I will punish the world for its evil, and the wicked for their iniquity; I will halt the arrogance of the proud..."'*

Ezekiel 30:1-3 *"Thus says the Lord God: 'Wail, "Woe to the day!" For the day is near, even the day of the Lord is near; it will be* **a day of clouds,** *the time of the Gentiles."*

Amos 5:18-20 *"Woe to you who desire the day of the Lord! For what good is the day of the Lord to you?* **It will be darkness,** *and not light. It will be as though a man fled from a lion, and a bear met him! Or as though he went into the house, leaned his hand on the wall, and a serpent bit him! Is not the day of the Lord darkness, and not light?* **Is it not very dark, with no brightness in it?"**

Matthew 24:29 *"Immediately after the distress of those days* **'the sun will be darkened, and the moon will not give its light; the stars will fall from the sky, and the heavenly bodies will be shaken."**

I have heard so many speculations as to what will cause the sun to be darkened and the moon to not give its light. I speculated for many years myself until I realised that the answers are right there in scripture. Revelations tell us why, *"I looked when He opened the sixth seal, and behold, there was a great earthquake; and the sun became black as sackcloth of hair, and the moon became like blood. And the stars of heaven fell to the earth, as a fig tree drops its late figs when it is shaken by a mighty wind."* Revelations 6:12-13 The dust and smoke released by a great earthquake blocked out the light from the sun and the moon.

This event coincided with a meteor shower that would have produced its own smoke and dust as these blazing heavenly bodies slams into the earth.

There are many other scriptures that speak of this day using similar descriptions but this also is around the time when God and man will go head to head.

Continue to the next chapter where we will look at the battle of Armageddon.

Chapter 5

Armageddon God and Man at War

Based on Joel Chapter 3

If the end time were to be seen as a 24 hour day, this is an idea of what that day would look like.

1. It would begin with the birth of Jesus
2. The ministry of John the Baptist and Jesus' preparation of those who would become the foundations of the Church would follow.
3. The next major event would be the death, burial, resurrection and ascension of Jesus.
4. After that would be the coming of the Holy Spirit and the birth of the Church.
5. Not long after would be the coming of the spirit of antichrist, the initial persecution of the Church and the scattering of God's people.
6. Things would then begin to intensify by the eve of the day. The forces of nature will begin to go out of control causing famines and earthquakes etc.
7. We would then see the beginning of the 'greats'; the great deception and the great falling away.
8. The event known as the abomination that maketh desolate will then take place triggering the anger of God and forcing the final

countdown to the end.
9. This event would mark the beginning of the great persecution against both Jew and Gentile believers.
10. God will now have to intervene before all His elect are killed. Strange things will begin to happen on the earth and to celestial elements as an indication that God is on His way. These include the darkening of the sun, the moon and the stars. Civilisation is now in its final hour.
11. This day would then close with the return of Jesus when He sends His angels to gather the elect. He will come to earth with His saints and armies of angels. He will go on to destroy with fire all who practice evil, their systems and structures.

Man at war with God

As we embark on chapter 3 of Joel we are immediately met with a 'God versus man' battle down in the Valley of Jehoshaphat. God is about to take His revenge upon mankind for what they did to His Son and people. Remember that whatever you do to God's people you are doing to God. Jesus said, *"Assuredly, I say to you, inasmuch as you did it to one of the least of these My brethren, you did it to Me."* Matthew 25:40 Jesus speaking about the last days in Luke chapter 17 said this, *"But first He [the Son of Man] must suffer many things and be rejected by this generation. And as it was in the days of Noah, so it will be also in the days of the Son of Man…"* Jesus spoke in the first person tense when describing the suffering of His people as if He was the one suffering. Rejecting and persecuting His people is synonymous to rejecting and persecuting Him. Paul, before his conversion, relentlessly persecuted God's people. Jesus, speaking from heaven, said this to him when He met him on the road to Damascus. *"Saul, Saul, why are you persecuting Me?"* Acts 9:3

Joel chapter 3 begins...

Joel 3:1-3
"In those days and at that time, when I restore the fortunes of Judah and Jerusalem, I will gather all nations and bring them down to the Valley of Jehoshaphat there I will enter into judgment against them concerning my inheritance, my people Israel, for they scattered my people among the nations and divided up my land. They cast lots for my people and traded boys for prostitutes; they sold girls for wine that they might drink..."

In the same breath that God spoke of bringing salvation to His people (restore the fortunes of Judah and Jerusalem) He speaks of the judgement He will meet out to His human adversaries in the Valley. The coming of God's salvation, Jesus, the sending of His Holy Spirit and the judgement of His enemies in the Valley of Jehoshaphat will take place in the same time period, the end times. As this book was being written the suffering and rejection of Jesus by all nations, even by so called Christian nations, was already well on the way. We are presently on the watch for an escalation of this suffering and rejection which will signal the beginning of the great tribulation[1] which will start with the ultimate suffering and rejection of God's people. It will be like persecution on steroids. When we see such things we will know the gathering of all nations (or the armies of all nations) down in the Valley of Jehoshaphat, or as mentioned in Revelation 16 'Armageddon' will soon take place.

It was man who brought the fight to God first. Not a single one of them will survive His response.

In both the Joel and Revelation accounts, this gathering for war is

---

[1] Jesus in Matthew 24:21 speaks of the great tribulation (KJV). The debate rages on as to whether God's people will go through this period. The answer is yes, 'this is the patience of the saints'.

mentioned. This could be the war that started with an attack on Jerusalem that culminated with the declaration to rid the earth of all God's people. So vicious will be this outright war against God through His people that God will have to respond and intervene to shorten the suffering of His elect. *"...unless those days were shortened, no flesh would be saved; but for the elect's sake those days will be shortened."* Matthew 25:22 I believe the 'no flesh' here is referring to God's people and not all the peoples of the earth. In other words, none of God's people would be left alive, so for our sake He shortened the days of our tribulation. God's intervention will be His answer to the world's evil against His people by sending trouble of His own to His persecutors. *"...He will pay back trouble to those who trouble you and give relief to you who are troubled..."* 2 Thessalonians 1:6-7

Joel 3:14
"Multitudes, multitudes in the valley of decision! For the day of the LORD is near in the valley of decision."

Revelation 16:14-15. *"They are spirits of demons performing miraculous signs, and they go out to the kings of the whole world, to gather them for the battle on the great day of God Almighty. 'Behold, I come like a thief! Blessed is he who stays awake and keeps his clothes with him, so that he may not go naked and be shamefully exposed.' Then they gathered the kings together to the place that in Hebrew is called Armageddon."*

Satan, in the midst of his efforts to rid the earth of God's people as he did with John the Baptist, Jesus and many of the apostles, gets news that causes him to gather his forces for a battle in the valley of decision, also called the valley of Jehoshaphat or Armageddon. *"But news from the east and the north shall trouble him; therefore he shall go out with great fury to destroy and annihilate many. And he shall plant the tents of his palace between the seas and the glorious holy mountain; yet he shall come to his end, and no one will help him. At that time Michael shall stand up, the great prince who stands watch over the sons of your people; and there shall be a time of trouble, such as never was since there was a nation, even to that time. And at that time your people shall be delivered, every one who is found written in the book."* Daniel 11:44-45 to 12:1 Heaven steps in to deliver the remnant of God's elect who were not yet slaughtered. God will bring the fight to those who brought the fight to Him when they troubled us but He will first take us out of the earth.

Joel 3:15-16 *"The Lord also shall roar out of Zion, and utter his voice from Jerusalem; and the heavens and the earth shall shake; but the Lord will be the hope of his people and the strength of the children of Israel."*

Revelation 16:18 *"Then there came flashes of lightning, rumblings, peals of thunder and a severe earthquake. No earthquake like it has ever occurred since man has been on earth, so tremendous was the quake."*

God's people Israel will first be attacked by an army. This attack was orchestrated by God as He uses it to judge and purge His people of the wickedness that had infiltrated their hearts. *"'Have you not brought this on yourself, in that you have forsaken the Lord your God when He led you in the way? ... Your own wickedness will correct you, and your backslidings will rebuke you. Know therefore and see that it is an evil and bitter thing that you have forsaken the Lord your God, and the fear of Me is not in you,' Says the Lord God of hosts."* Jeremiah 2:17-19

In the midst of this onslaught however, God's people repent and turn to Him, so God has mercy on them and turns to destroy the armies He gathered to trouble them. Zechariah's account seems to confirm this. *"A day of the LORD is coming when your plunder will be divided among you. I will gather all the nations to Jerusalem to fight against it; the city will be captured, the houses ransacked, and the women raped.*

Half of the city will go into exile, but the rest of the people will not be taken from the city. Then the LORD will go out and fight against those nations, as he fights in the day of battle. On that day his feet will stand on the Mount of Olives, east of Jerusalem, and the Mount of Olives will be split in two from east to west, forming a great valley, with half of the mountain moving north and half moving south. You will flee by my mountain valley, for it will extend to Azel. You will flee as you fled from the earthquake in the days of Uzziah king of Judah. Then the LORD my God will come, and all the holy ones with him." Zechariah 14:1-5

"At that time his voice shook the earth, but now he has promised, 'Once more I will shake not only the earth but also the heavens.' The words 'once more' indicate the removing of what can be shaken—that is, created things—" Hebrews 12:26-27

From 2 Chronicles 20, the following facts emerge. Jehoshaphat, whose name means "Yahweh will judge", witnessed a battle which required no fighting by His people. Forces led by Ammon, Moab and Mt. Seir had assembled in Engedi against Judah. The people of Judah were in great fear and gathered with Jehoshaphat before the Temple in Jerusalem to pray and seek Yahweh's help.

This account seemed to resemble the same format where God sends human armies against His people to judge them but then turns against these armies when His people repents. The salvation of His people then came in the form of a victory earned by God's own doing and not by the people. Could it be, that we are about to see a repeat of this in the valley of decision/Jehoshaphat/Armageddon?

Joel 3:17-21 After the terrible events of these days (and the return of Jesus), Joel's prophecy indicates that there will be a time of peace where God will rule the earth from Jerusalem. This could be the time of the millennial reign or the beginning of eternity where we will have new heavens and a new earth.

Remember that what we know as 'time' was something triggered by sin. Eternity continued until sin entered and started a count down to the judgement when sin would be dealt with by God. Time is a reminder that God will soon judge sinners. Only the earthen body of a believer is subject to time, our spirits have already entered eternity. Jesus said, *"...whoever lives and believes in Me shall never die."* John 11:26 That is, if our spirits have been brought to life through Jesus, we will never experience the true death, for real death is not a physical experience but a spiritual one.

Conclusion
The mere volume of prophetic utterances warning about this coming wrath is clear sign that it must not be taken lightly. God sent salvation to the world, all who cry out to God need only now to receive Him, who is Jesus the Messiah. Do it before the end of the age and the time of the hardening of men's heart. Do it now.

Years ago when I was convicted by the truth of scriptures I prayed a prayer similar to this one. "Jesus, I acknowledge that I am a sinner worthy of hell. Please forgive me and come into my heart and save me. I believe You are the Christ, Son of the living God, the only One through whom I can receive forgiveness of sins and inherit eternal life."

Soon after bowing my heart in prayer and brokenness for the sins I had committed against God I began to experience the power of God's forgiveness and the regeneration of my soul.

If you have been convicted by what you have read so far you might want to pray a prayer similar to the one I prayed. It doesn't matter if you are a believer or a nonbeliever, if you are convicted turn to God now and you will experience the miracle of His salvation and transforming power. You need only to truly believe and truly repent from your heart and God will give you the 'Gift of Faith' that will give you the power to obey His word.

Chapter 6

Part 2: It's Here

The Great Falling Away
Before The Abomination

Based on Matthew Chapter 24:1-14

Snake For Dinner?
I watched the video of the two little children, obviously from some remote third world country, farming snakes. The little boy was about eight and his sister about 11 years old. He had placed the lower part of his little body down into the snake's hole as a bait for the snake to wrap itself around. His upper body from chest up was left out. After the snake wrapped itself around him, he used his exposed arms to pull himself up, with the help of his sister. He is now on the ground untangling himself from a massive, over 15 ft, snake. With his sister's help he is finally untangled so he gathers up the live snake and they move on to their next catch. The snakes in this region were obviously not venomous.

This time the sister sprang into action. A smaller opening was an indication that this snake was not as big so she went to work with a hoe digging further along where she estimated the hole tunneled. Soon she exposed an opening further along the tunnel and the side of another snake inside. Her brother rest the large seemingly stunned snake down and they both took hold on to this other snake and pulled it out the hole. This one looked just over 10 ft. and was small enough to hold in a large mesh sack she carried. They retrieved another one of similar size in a similar way within the same location while keeping an eye, sometimes a hand or a foot, on the one that was too large to hold in the sack. The video ended with the two smaller snakes writhing in the sack that the sister carried and the large one folded over and down between both arms of the little brother as they happily headed off with their catch.

As I watched these two little bare footed children in tattered clothing bravely labouring for what will become their meal, I could not help but compare them with our modern, Western World children. I remembered the last time I visited Canada and heard the tragic news of a young teenage girl who committed suicide because her parents would not allow her to go to the concert of one of her favourite pop stars. I remember my frustration as a college tutor dealing with learners who did no work but thought they had some entitlement to still succeed. I observed other tutors and even department heads cheat on their behalf to give them success they did not earn. I remember my own children who were always complaining that there is nothing in the house to eat, which really meant there was nothing already prepared that they could just microwave or eat right from a packet.

In the case of a global economic and technological meltdown which of the two groups of children would be able to survive? The answer is obviously those poor resourceful Third World Country children who can feed themselves without money or technology. They have the skills to survive without gas, piped water, electricity or even adult help?

The youths and many adults of the First World would not fare so well. **You see, the prosperity of the West will no doubt be its undoing. It has made us the slaves of comfort and convenience.** The result is a generation of mostly self absorbed and lazy children who would go into shock if their mobile phone's network stopped working. They are so soft they, for the most part, would gladly hand over their rights and souls at the promise of keeping their comforts in times of tribulation. I am here talking about 'Christian' youths as well.

The massive global reset is here. Nature and society as we know it is about to radically change. Are you ready to live without access to money and technology? The time has come for us to begin preparing ourselves to live like those snake hunting children, without money or electronic technology.

The End According to Jesus

In part 1 of this book we looked at the prophet Joel's account of the last days but now in part 2 we will continue by looking at the account of the greatest prophet that ever lived, Jesus. We will discover that Jesus' account will agree with Joel's account but will also highlight additional events that weren't mentioned by Joel. Joel spoke of the events in nature and the attack upon God's people that would signal the end. Jesus mentions these also but then went on to put the spotlight on the changes that would take place in the hearts and attitudes of men. These include the increase in deception and the abomination that will trigger the final countdown to the return of Jesus and the desolation of the whole earth.

Matthew 24:1-3 - The temple's fate

"Jesus left the temple and was walking away when his disciples came up to him to call his attention to its buildings. 'Do you see all these things?' he asked. 'Truly I tell you, not one stone here will be left on another;

everyone will be thrown down.' As Jesus was sitting on the Mount of Olives, the disciples came to him privately. 'Tell us,' they said, 'when will this happen, and what will be the sign of your coming and of the end of the age?'"

Jesus' disciples wanted clear markers that would signal not just the fate of the wonderful temple but the end of time itself so they asked Him about the signs that will signify the end. Jesus in His answer went on to describe events that would lead up to the 'day of the Lord'. He tells them about the natural disasters that would indicate the beginning of the end. He told them about famines and wars as Joel did, but then He also told them about deception and the great falling away, things Joel did not mention. Yes, human driven tragedies and natural disasters will be happening in unparalleled proportion and intensity but one would do well to note that, of all these, He spoke more about deception than anything else. I refer to these as, 'The Double Decker sandwich of deception', three layers of warnings about deception with other things in between. Jesus warned us about deception at the beginning, in the middle and towards the end of His end times predictions. Jesus, the greatest prophet of all times, thought it most important to highlight this very significant sign posts and we should take note.

DECEPTION WARNING LAYER 1
Many among the masses are deceivers so watch out that no one deceives you

Matthew 24:4-5
"Jesus answered: 'Watch out that no one deceives you. For many will come in my name, claiming, 'I am the Messiah,' and will deceive many.'"

The ASV translation says it this way, *"And Jesus answered and said unto them, Take heed that no man lead you astray. For many shall come in my name, saying, I am the Christ; and shall lead many astray."*

Jesus opened up His answer to the disciple's question by describing the first layer of deception. He spoke of the great many who will bare His name but lie about their knowledge of Him or relationship with Him. The fact that He began on this topic is an indication of its importance. "Watch out..", He says. This is a warning as well as a command. He is telling us to be on the lookout. What are we looking for? We are looking for MANY deceivers, not a few. These deceivers will have a claim. What Jesus says about their claim could be interpreted in two ways. 1. These individuals claim that they are Jesus. This interpretation is the most popular and is hinted at by how the Knew King James version pountuates it. 2. These individuals rightly claim that Jesus is the Messiah. Imagine Jesus pointing to Himself as He spoke those words *"For many shall come in my name, saying, I* [Jesus] *am the Christ."*

I would like to suggest that the first interpretation is incorrect. Why? History has proven that the number of those who were crazy enough to claim they were the Jesus of the bible were only a few. They weren't able to have much of a following either. Jesus said there would be many making the claim and many who would be deceived by them.

I want to put forth the second interpretation to be the correct one. Why? Those who come in the name of Christ today number in the millions. They say they are 'CHRISTians' and do acknowledge that Jesus is the promised Messiah but are only using this claim to get in among us to exploit us. Jesus says, *"These people draw near to Me with their mouth, and honor Me with their lips, but their heart is far from Me."* Matthew 15:8 Again in Matthew 7:21-22 Jesus explains that many who acknowledge Him as Lord will not enter His kingdom. I have never known anyone who claimed they were Jesus and those whom I have heard of would not have fooled me. I have a few times however been deceived and made a fool of by people who claimed they were one of us. They said they were 'Christians' and fooled and exploited myself and many others.

Paul the apostle spoke about the last days by describing the wickedness of deception that will mark these times, the very deception that we must be on the lookout for. He said, "...*evildoers and impostors will go from bad to worse, deceiving and being deceived.*" Timothy 3:13 Please remember that this is just the beginning of Jesus' answer, He will again warn us to be on our guard against deception in our time. The deceivers spoken of here are the many antichrists/false Christians that are preparing the way for the well renowned and much spoken of Antichrist himself. The man who will be the very embodiment of lies and head of Mystery Babylon the counterfeit Church.

1. Not all Israel is Israel
"For they are not all Israel, which are of Israel..." Romans 9:6
Has it dawned on you yet that there are saved Christians as well as unsaved Christians? That Christianity is a title worn by all kinds? For years I tried to consider everyone who went by that title a brother or sister but something just wasn't adding up. It was clear to anyone who was willing to admit the truth that many of these people did not know God or love Him. In fact, many were the enemies of the cross who stood in the way blocking the work of the Lord.

There are many things said in scripture that confirm this truth, some said by Jesus Himself. In one of His renowned parables Jesus started out by saying, *"The kingdom of heaven is like a man who sowed good seed in his field..."* Matthew 13:24-30 He then continued to explain how an enemy then came in and planted tares or weeds in the master's field. The problem with tares is that they look exactly like wheat while without fruit. One would not be able to tell the difference until they began to blossom and put out fruit. The tares spoken of in this parable are believed to be the plant known as Darnel today. Wikipedia compares it to wheat. "The similarity between these two plants is so great that in some regions, darnel is referred to as "false wheat". It bears a close resemblance to wheat until the ear appears."[1]

We can safely conclude therefore, that not all the plants in God's field are wheat. Some are weeds planted by the devil, crowding, choking and robbing the true wheat of necessary nutrients. They are nonproductive pollutants that creates hassle and confusion. The kingdom currently has two types in it, one pure and undefiled the other putrid and rotten.

Paul in another place uses the analogy of vessels in a master's house. He said some vessels were honourable. No doubt these would be delightfully used by the master Himself as well as to serve guests. Another group of vessels however, were fit to be used only for menial tasks or not fit to be used at all, ready to be thrown out onto the garbage heap. Maybe they were cracked, chipped or stained etc. If you have ever been to a potter's yard you may remember seeing a heap of broken pottery. Rejects that were splintered and piled onto a heap to be dumped. Similarly, God is pleased by some but totally ashamed of others who bear His name.

2. Not all who verbalise it live it

Jesus said, *"Not all those who say 'You are our Lord' will enter the kingdom of heaven. The only people who will enter the kingdom of heaven are those who do what my Father in heaven wants."* Matthew 7:21 (NCV)

This one needs no explanation. Obviously this teaches us that talk is cheap. Faith cannot be judged by what a person says alone, as many

---

[1] https://en.wikipedia.org/wiki/Lolium_temulentum

will say all the right things while refusing TO DO the right thing. They will not enter the kingdom.

This should be no surprise as we have been seeing examples of this over thousands of years. Consider the following.

3. Not all of God's people who left Egypt under the leadership of Moses entered Canaan.

4. Not all of Lot's family who left Sodom entered Zoar. His wife died on the way because her heart was in the wrong place.

Paul speaking by the inspiration of the Holy Spirit gave this instruction to the Corinthian Church, *"Examine yourselves to see whether you are in the faith; test yourselves."* 2 Corinthians 13:5a James speaking to God's people wrote: *"You adulterous people, don't you know that friendship with the world means enmity against God? Therefore, anyone who chooses to be a friend of the world becomes an enemy of God... Submit yourselves, then, to God. Resist the devil, and he will flee from you. Come near to God and he will come near to you. Wash your hands, you sinners, and purify your hearts, you double-minded. Grieve, mourn and wail. Change your laughter to mourning and your joy to gloom. Humble yourselves before the Lord, and he will lift you up."* James 4:4-10 The fact is that those who persecuted, planned and executed the eventual death of Christ were religious people who said they were God's instruments. They paid tithes, fasted and prayed, they wore all the right religious garments, observed all the religious feasts and regularly attended the house of God but then went and planned how they could trap and kill Jesus. As it was then so shall it be in the end.

Matthew 24:6-7a The Wars Without
You *"...will hear of wars and rumors of wars, but see to it that you are not*

alarmed. Such things must happen, but the end is still to come. Nation will rise against nation, and kingdom against kingdom."

Where people's heart and attitudes turn away from the values and truth of Christ who is the, 'Prince of Peace', you will no doubt find a lot of fighting.*"For where you have envy and selfish ambition, there you find disorder and every evil practice."* James 3:16 Envy and selfish ambition are only two of the many destructive traits that will fill the hearts and attitudes of people in our times. There will therefore, most certainly be betrayals and wars as Jesus spoke of in Matthew 24. James himself continued to describe in chapter 4:1 that fights and quarrels are the result of such self centred attitudes. The beginning of the end will be marked with wars and rumours of wars among nations headed by prime ministers and presidents etc. and also among kingdoms headed by monarchs. The fact that Jesus mentions it means that the activities will be beyond what would be considered normal.

Matthew 24:7b Natural disasters
"There will be famines and earthquakes in various places." We must never ignore the fact that these natural disasters could very well be man made. Famines caused by greed and earthquakes possibly caused by human experiments and tampering with nature.

Matthew 24:9 & 14 Persecution that will eventually aid the spreading of the gospel
"Then you will be handed over to be persecuted and put to death, and you will be hated by all nations because of me… And this gospel of the kingdom will be preached in the whole world as a testimony to all nations, and then the end will come."

Normal Persecution
Persecution is nothing new to the church. This persecution that Jesus

predicted started from the very birth of the church as recorded in the book of Acts. Back then the main perpetrators were Jewish leaders who wanted to quash the great increase in the numbers of Jesus followers. As we approach the end of days this persecution will again flare up but will this time be worldwide and enforced mainly by Gentile peoples.

Consider this new perspective as to the cause of the now global hatred of the Lord and His people and the persecution that will ensue. Consider the possibility that one of the main reasons can be found in the first statement Jesus made in His answer to the disciples. *"Watch out that no one deceives you, many will come in my name, claiming, 'I am the Messiah,' and will deceive many."* We can see traces of dislike and complete rejection of Jesus and the Christian cause in even European countries like the United Kingdom, Sweden and Holland presently. This mistrust was because many who came in the name of Christ were found out to be deceivers, hypocrites, paedophiles, users and abusers of people.

If for example, you should have three or four consecutive bad experiences with the police you could easily write off all police because of those experiences never trusting them again. The devil plants his deceivers in our midst to discredit the name of Christ and block the path to Jesus. One of the meanings of anti is to 'stand in the place of.' A big part of the great deception is the lie that says Christianity is nothing more than a group of deceiving hypocrites using religion to advance their own evil agendas. These deceivers have caused wide scale mistrust of anyone who comes in the name of the Lord, a mistrust that is changing to hatred as the devil intensifies his strategy.

"But there were also false prophets among the people, even as there will be false teachers among you, who will secretly bring in destructive heresies, even denying the Lord who bought them, and bring on themselves swift

*destruction. And many will follow their destructive ways, **because of whom the way of truth will be blasphemed.*** " 2 Peter 2:1-2

Others will hate us because we refuse to act and speak in the world's way. The world is drunk on their religion of 'social justice'. They have received a very strong delusion which says love is synonymous with inclusion. They believe including everyone no matter what religion, sexual orientation, morality etc. is a demonstration of love, which means they are of God, for peace and good. God's standards of holiness and righteousness however are not open to be reinterpreted by man, God alone is God. To be politically correct is not the same as being Biblically correct.

Increased Decadence Without
As the world sinks deeper into this demon induced acceptance of other beliefs and sins of compulsion (people who cannot help themselves) their self righteousness will cause them to burn with hatred for the 'exclusive people', those of us who hold to the truth of scriptures declaring plainly and without hesitation that Jesus is the only salvation and those who live and die in sin will not inherit the kingdom of God but will be tormented forever in a burning hell. People who truly love God will be labelled as haters and warmongers because they hold fast to their confession and will not conform to the new popular norms. Their theory of inclusion and social justice will somehow exclude and be totaly unjust to us.

The devil is already rounding up his people who are outside the Church. The advent of global satellite communications coupled with fast international travel has for the first time introduced global interconnections that has also made global wars and law enforcement possible. The world is already uniting under certain ideologies and moralities and will soon unite under a single leader and currency.

For example, the United States number one export is its values. These values, for the most part, were spread abroad through the captivating power of Hollywood. The US especially, has used its global TV news networks to help to shape the opinions of the masses rather than just inform them. Now their mobile and social network giants are harvesting our personal data at alarming rates. Global influence is now a reality and global power is now consolidating. We see this happening with global conglomerates pushing local and smaller entrepreneurs out of business. After the 'big fishes' have eaten up all the 'little fishes' they will have complete consumer control. At this point they will be able to greatly influence or even dictate how and what we consume, be it information or food.

Take for example what is happening in Japan today. This country with its deeply traditional culture bypassed its many beautiful and tasty dishes to adopt KFC as its new traditional Christmas meal.[1] How could an American company be able to reach so deeply into the hearts and minds of a nation with such strong traditional values? Do not be deceived, there are corporations today that are much more powerful than many nations. Do not underestimate their power. Consolidated, centralised power removes freedom of choice from the people and creates dictators. Power will become so consolidated that the whole world will soon answer to one man.

Matthew 24:14
"And this gospel of the kingdom will be preached in the whole world as a testimony to all nations.."

I have heard television evangelists and owners of Christian television networks say that the preaching of the gospel to the whole earth as

---

[1] http://www.bbc.com/capital/story/20161216-why-japan-celebrates-christmas-with-kfc

described by Jesus will be as a result of Christian television reaching the globe through satellite transmissions. I beg to disagree. For one, I have often seen preaching on these networks that are not consistent with 'the gospel' but are doctrines of devils spoken by deceivers. Jesus spoke of a specific gospel calling it 'this gospel of the Kingdom' not some other 'gospel' conjured up by the imaginations of carnal minds that esteem the desires and convenience of men above obedience to Christ. Paul acknowledges the existence of these other messages *"I am astonished that you are so quickly deserting the one who called you to live in the grace of Christ and are turning to a different gospel..."* Galatians 1:6

All kinds of 'gospels' have already been preached to the world but 'this gospel of the Kingdom' that Jesus refers to is yet to be heard by everyone. Due to our sinful tendencies it is very difficult for the gospel in its purest form to be proclaimed in our times of prosperity and comfort. It takes the heat of persecution to strip away the flesh and carnality from our message and this is what, no doubt, will happen in these end times when we will have global enforcement of persecution for people of true Christ centred faith. The news of the 'heretics' who will prefer death or imprisonment rather than deny their faith will spread like wildfire. As we are seen and interviewed on international news networks the world will be made aware of and again faced with our cause, which is the gospel message of Jesus our saviour.

As stated in Mark's account this is the time we will again *"...stand before governors and kings as witnesses to them"* (Mark 13:9) as they consider our fate whether to pardon us or enforce capital punishment. As Jesus stood before Pilate so will we stand before governors while the people shout 'crucify them'. Remember this would not be the first time we are seeing the pivotal role persecution plays in the proliferation of the gospel as it was also the case at the beginning of the Church age.

Jesus Himself, Paul and other Apostles were brought before governors, judges and political leaders and asked about their cause. In their answer they were able to declare the message of the cross.

When we are brought before these people Jesus said we should not worry about what we should say, *"Whenever you are arrested and brought to trial, do not worry beforehand about what to say. Just say whatever is given you at the time, for it is not you speaking, but the Holy Spirit."* Mark 13:11 Read the book of the Acts of the Apostles. Paul the Apostle himself was able to share the gospel with governors, soldiers and fellow prisoners while he was persecuted and in bonds. A classic example was when the first martyr of the Church age Stephen, was brought before the Sanhedrin where he spoke the message of Jesus boldly. As it happened with Stephen so shall it happen to us. International persecution during this period will bring opportunities for the gospel that would not normally be available. Joel spoke of the suffering that would be meted out to God's people but did not mention the increased deception that would creep in among us.

DECEPTION WARNING LAYER 2
Leaders and preachers who are deceivers
Matthew 24:10-12
*"At that time many will turn away from the faith and will betray and hate each other, and **many false prophets** will appear and deceive many people. Because of the increase of wickedness, the love of most will grow cold..."*

Those outside are easy pickings for the devil so his attention is focussed on us who are within. Jesus now explains a main source of deception among His people. A rise of deception will come from the rise in false prophets. These false prophets will arise during the time of trouble when offense and betrayal are mainstream in God's Church just before the time of great persecution. Of the prophecies given by Jesus and His disciples this one seems to shout the loudest. Jesus, having explained what would happen in nature, nations and kingdoms now continues by telling us about what would happen among His people.

Wars within - betrayal and the increase of wickedness
There will be religious deception, a falling away from the truth and a rise in competitive Christianity and mistrust that will result in infightings etc. *"At that time many will fall away and will betray one another and hate one another."* Matthew 24:10 (NASB) What are they falling away from? They are falling away from the faith and from truth. Who are they betraying and hating? Each other. What is a main reason for this falling away? False doctrines taught by false prophets.

Paul speaking of the same event said, the apostasy or rebellion must happen before the day of the Lord comes. *"Let no one deceive you by any means; for that Day will not come unless the falling away comes first, and the man of sin is revealed, the son of perdition..."* 2 Thessalonians 2:3 Apostasy means: The abandonment or renunciation of a religious or political belief or principle. (Oxford Dictionary)

A massive falling away or renunciation of the true faith (possibly not in a very obvious way) was destined to take place. No question about it, we are witnessing it presently. Paul again speaks of this event. *"But the Spirit explicitly says that in later times some will fall away from the faith, paying attention to deceitful spirits and **doctrines of demons**..."* 1 Timothy 4:1

Scriptures spoke several times about this sad time. Paul told Timothy about it in both his first and second letters to him. In his second letter he said this, *"I solemnly charge you in the presence of God and of Christ*

*Jesus, who is to judge the living and the dead, and by His appearing and His kingdom: preach the word; be ready in season and out of season; reprove, rebuke, exhort, with great patience and instruction. For the time will come when they will not endure sound doctrine; but wanting to have their ears tickled, they will accumulate for themselves **teachers in accordance to their own desires,** and will turn away their ears from the truth and will turn aside to myths."* 2 Timothy 4:1-4

Please note that one needs to put up with or endure sound doctrine because sound doctrine demands obedience to a master, even our Lord. Sound doctrine can make us very uncomfortable and are many times not convenient in a time when convenience marks the way of the world. People in these times will prefer to listen to doctrines of devils that caters to their carnality than listen to the truth that demands purity, self control and faith in God.

The verses that speak of this falling away are too numerous for this one chapter but let us look again at one I quoted earlier. Peter says, *"But there were also **false prophets among the people,** even as there will be false teachers among you, who will secretly bring in destructive heresies, even denying the Lord who bought them, and bring on themselves swift destruction. And many will follow their destructive ways, because of whom the way of truth will be blasphemed. By covetousness they will exploit you with deceptive words…"* 2 Peter 2:1-3

Deception in our Time

Many of the Jewish converts, who found it difficult to separate the requirement of Moses' law from the new way through Jesus Christ, were insisting that Gentile believers should be circumcised. God's appointed leaders therefore, had to come together as a council to pray, consider and settle the issue of what God required of Gentiles who came to faith and were now joining the commonwealth of Israel. This sums up their answer... *"For it seemed good to the Holy Spirit, and to us, to lay upon you no greater burden than these necessary things: that you abstain from things offered to idols, from blood, from things strangled, and from sexual immorality. If you keep yourselves from these, you will do well."* Acts 15:28-29. Let us explain, for a moment, the significance of this statement.

In other words, the Gentiles should not be burdened by any of Moses' laws but only be careful to not bring elements of their pagan culture over into their new found faith. Very important and therefore needed stating. *"...abstain from things offered to idols, from blood, from things strangled, and from sexual immorality."* Why? Just as the legalistic burdens of the Jewish religion must be resisted by Gentile converts, similarly the pagan practices of their former worship must be resisted. It is a great temptation for Jews to go back to putting their faith in the law but the greater temptation for Gentiles is reverting to paganism. The Jews rejection of Christ opened the way for Gentile believers so we are living in the time of a predominantly Gentile Church. When Gentile believers fall away they revert to their old ways, paganism, witchcraft and atheism. Today we are witnessing Gentile believers in their masses returning to their pagan roots while still professing faith in Christ. Again the power of global television networks are pivotal in spreading the message that fuels the rise of paganism in the Church.

Have you noticed the rise in sexual immorality among ministers and professing 'Christians'? Listen what Jesus said, *"Many will say to Me in that day, 'Lord, Lord, have we not prophesied in Your name, cast out demons in Your name, and done many wonders in Your name?' And then I will declare to them, 'I never knew you; depart from Me, you who practice lawlessness!'"* Matthew 7:22-23. Pagan 'Christians' working false miracles in the name of Jesus by the power of their pagan gods (Jeremiah 2:8). There is an influx of all that is false and pagan into the Church today. This is nothing new, the Roman Church split with the Eastern Orthodox Church for over 800 years now. During their dominance of the Medieval Realms the Roman Church under Emperor Constantine, in order to pacify the local pagan leaders considered the political expediency of empire building rather than the efficacy of the pure gospel. They therefore, mixed pagan practices into Christianity under the guise of Church festivals. The pure truths that were passed down to God's people are polluted by pagan practises, producing an anaemic and frail step-child that does not have the DNA of GOD. It is the progenitor of the abomination that maketh desolate! It has been sired and tutored by demons.

Charismatic Witchcraft The New 'Christianity'
This group of Gentile converts who are reverting to paganism has been the most deceptive since time began, hence Jesus' warning, *"For false christs and false prophets will rise and show great signs and wonders to deceive, if possible, even the elect. See, I have told you beforehand."* Matthew 24:24-25. They will have all the outward look and boast all the 'spiritual' experiences but are rebels. This is the mystery of iniquity, where children of devils boast all the spiritual experiences and manifest all the spiritual power gifts but they are not of the Holy Spirit. We struggle to get our heads around it. As the seven sons of Sceva tried to use the power vested in the name of Jesus without having a relationship with Him in the same way these will use the power vested in God's word while in rebellion against God. They practice 'Charismatic witchcraft'. They love the benefits associated with the kingdom of God but do not sincerely love the King Himself and therefore refuse to obey His will.

Let's look again at Paul's prophecy concerning the great falling away as recorded in 2 Thessalonians 2:3 *"Let no one deceive you by any means; for that Day will not come unless the falling away comes first, and the man of sin is revealed, the son of perdition…"* Some translations call him 'the man of lawlessness'. Lawless means disobedient or one who will not conform to the law, a rebel. Note that in God's eyes rebellion and witchcraft are one in the same. *"For rebellion is as the sin of witchcraft, and stubbornness is as iniquity and idolatry. Because you have rejected the word of the Lord, He also has rejected you..."* 1 Samuel 15:23

The falling away from the faith and from truth and the infiltration of pagan worship and witchcraft into 'Christianity', introduced by workers of iniquity (Matthew 7:23 (KJV)), was prophesied by Jesus and His apostles. We today are witnessing it with wide eyes and dropped jaws.

The prosperity doctrine, the compulsion to tithe, the confession and declaration movement, the hyper grace doctrine, commanding of angels and the many non verifiable counterfeit faith healings are but only a few examples. These teachings are thematically consistent in removing the preeminence of Jesus Christ as Lord and King and showcasing 'Christian' celebrities while placing the emphasis on man's desires, standards and abilities.

On one end of the spectrum we have the more vibrant supposedly 'spirit filled' evangelical believers heading down the path of sorcery while on the other end we have those that are dead, motionless and empty. Many of these 'liberal's have services in massive, old, cold stone buildings with congregations that struggle to grow beyond five or ten people. They do not believe in the biblical promise of the 'baptism in the Holy Ghost', in fact, they disregard great portions of scripture replacing them with their own rituals and rules. They are the ones ordaining homosexuals as priests/ministers and replacing the masculine references to God in scripture with gender neutral ones etc.

So, Jesus has now given His second warning about end time deception. His first was about those who said they were Christians but are liars. The second was about false preachers, those who claim to be messengers of God but are liars. The fact that what He says about deceiving false prophets, follows straight on in the same sentence where He speaks of the falling away from the faith, could mean that the false prophets will have much to do with this falling away. False prophets leading God's people astray.

How does a person who has fallen away from the faith look? We could immediately think they would have nothing more to do with religion, rather they would be going to clubs and avoiding religion. Would you imagine them in suites, carrying big bibles, with titles such as prophet, evangelist or apostle and getting many invitations to speak to large gatherings of God's people? Such deceivers could themselves be deceived into thinking that they are still in the faith not realising that they have fallen away. How many of those ministers we see on network TV today are still in the faith? Deception in our time is a provoking reality.

End of the Gentile Age
Paul made a statement in Roman 11 that is very disturbing, he said, *"For I do not desire, brethren, that you should be ignorant of this mystery, lest you should be wise in your own opinion, that blindness in part has happened to Israel until the fullness of the Gentiles has come in."* Roman 11:25 This is a mystery no believer should be ignorant of.

There have been other mysteries that are now clearly understood. The fact that God would open a way for Gentiles to share in the promises and inheritance of Israel was a great mystery in Old Testament times. Paul explains, *"...by revelation He made known to me the mystery (as I have briefly written already, by which, when you read, you may understand my knowledge in the mystery of Christ), which in other ages was not made known to the sons of men, as it has now been revealed by the Spirit to His holy apostles and prophets: that the Gentiles should be fellow heirs, of the same body, and partakers of His promise in Christ through the gospel..."* Ephesians 3:3-6

That mystery is now matched by this other mystery as mentioned in Romans 11 i.e. *"...blindness in part has happened to Israel until the fullness of the Gentiles has come in."* We understand this mystery to mean that the door opened to the Gentiles will not be opened indefinitely. There is a limit to the duration of its opening and to the number that will enter in. After that set number of Gentiles have entered into salvation hardness will take complete hold of the hearts of the non-Jewish people just as it once took hold of the Jews. We believe that at this time the paradigm will shift again where the eyes of the Jews will be opened to see and accept their messiah while the gentiles will want to have nothing to do with Him. This shift to paganism among the Gentile Churches signals the end of the Gentile Age.

God will use the persecution of these times to serve His purpose. It will be His way of sifting, purging and separating the true believers from the false. We will not know what material our faith is until it is put to the test by fire. Will it be found to be gold, silver or precious stone that is refined by fire or will it be found to be wood, hay or stubble that are consumed in fire?

We will look at deception layer 3 in the next chapter.

"Remember, I'm telling you this beforehand!" Matthew 24:25 (NTE)

Chapter 7

The Great Tribulation
God Judges His People

"For the time has come for judgment to begin at the house of God; and if it begins with us first, what will be the end of those who do not obey the gospel of God?" 1 Peter 4:17

Based on Matthew Chapter 24:15-29

Matthew 24:15 The abomination that brings desolation
"So when you see standing in the holy place 'the abomination that causes desolation,' spoken of through the prophet Daniel..."

What picture comes to mind when we think of abomination and desolation? Abomination means: a thing that causes disgust or loathing. Desolation means: a state of complete emptiness or destruction (Oxford Dictionary). Let us quote the above passage again but inserting the meaning of the words abomination and desolation to help understanding. "So when you see standing in the holy place the disgusting person/thing that causes emptiness or destruction..."

It would seem, from what Jesus is saying, that an absolutely disgusting thing or person will be set up or erected in the place that should be holy and set apart to God. God will be so offended by this thing that His intense dislike and disgust for that thing (or person) will greatly anger Him. The pouring out of His wrath will not be held back for much longer. The countdown will now begin. Nothing can survive God's wrath, there will be complete destruction that will leave the whole earth desolate and barren. According to Romans 2:9 Trouble will first come to the Jews then to the Gentiles so the destruction will begin in Israel before spreading to the rest of the world.

Some think that this abomination could be some homosexual act committed by the Antichrist in the newly erected Jewish temple on the Dome of the Rock. There is a possibility it could simply be the Jews, as a nation, bowing down and joining the pagan world in giving to the devil incarnate (the Antichrist) the worship that is due to Jesus. 2 Thessalonians 2 seems to suggest this. Having missed Jesus their true Messiah, Judaism that has managed to remain exclusive all these many years will possibly throw in their lot to become part of the world religion and give worship to the Antichrist thinking he is the messiah they long awaited. The Jews as a nation declaring Jesus' main rival, the Antichrist, as their long awaited messiah will no doubt awaken the indignation of God.

Matthew 24:16-21 Those in Judea fleeing to the mountains

"...then let those who are in Judea flee to the mountains. Let no one on the housetop go down to take anything out of the house. Let no one in the field go back to get their cloak. How dreadful it will be in those days for pregnant women and nursing mothers! Pray that your flight will not take place in winter or on the Sabbath. For then there will be great distress, unequaled from the beginning of the world until now—and never to be equaled again."

In the chapter before we spoke about normal persecution but this abomination will signal the beginning of the great persecution of God's people. There will be distress unequalled since the beginning of time as God uses the nations to punish Israel. Jesus' instruction therefore, is directed to those living in Judea as all who are in the plains will be killed by a cruel death beyond anything ever imagined or used in warfare before. As this will happen very shortly after the abomination is revealed there will be no time to delay for safety will only be found in the seclusion of the mountains. This is not the day of the Lord when God will rain destruction upon the whole earth, this is the work of men unleashing unparalleled destruction upon the Jews. This will coincide with an all out war against God's people worldwide.

This is coming from the hand of God as He uses others to punish and purge wickedness from among His people. A mechanism and machinery specifically designed to find and take out specific individuals will be created. Without God's intervention, none of God's people Jews or Gentile would survive. *"A voice is announcing from Dan, proclaiming disaster from the hills of Ephraim. "Tell this to the nations, proclaim concerning Jerusalem: 'A besieging army is coming from a distant land, raising a war cry against the cities of Judah. They surround her like men guarding a field, because she has rebelled against me,'" declares the Lord.* ***"Your own conduct and actions have brought this on you. This is your punishment. How bitter it is! How it pierces to the heart!"*** Jeremiah 4:15-18 (NIV)

Luke's account is a little bit clearer on this, *"When you see Jerusalem being surrounded by armies, you will know that its desolation is near. Then let those who are in Judea flee to the mountains, let those in the city get out, and let those in the country not enter the city."* Luke 21: 20 There will be a build up of armies around Jerusalem with the single intent of wiping Israel off the map.

Matthew 24:22-29 Great distress as never seen in the history of mankind

"If those days had not been cut short, no one would survive, but for the sake of the elect those days will be shortened. At that time if anyone says to you, 'Look, here is the Messiah!' or, 'There he is!' do not believe it. For false messiahs and false prophets will appear and perform great signs and wonders to deceive, if possible, even the elect. See, I have told you in advance. So if anyone tells you, 'There he is, out in the desert,' do not go out; or, 'Here he is, in the inner rooms,' do not believe it. For as lightning that comes from the east is visible even in the west, so will be the coming of the Son of Man. Wherever there is a carcass, there the vultures will gather. Immediately after the distress of those days the sun will be darkened, and the moon will not give its light; the stars will fall from the sky, and the heavenly bodies will be shaken."

So terrible will be these times that God will have to shorten what I believe will be the number of days that such events could prolong into. For example, if such days could go on over a period of eight months He will, for the sake of His suffering children, see to it that it wraps up within say four months otherwise none of His people would be left alive. Contrary to what some may think, God is indeed interested in the longevity of His children and humanity, He is not happy when there is pain, suffering and death. The devil will go all out against God and His people before the Lord replies in even greater measure. *"Now when the thousand years have expired, Satan will be released from his prison and will go out to deceive the nations which are in the four corners of the earth, Gog and Magog, to gather them together to battle, whose number is as the sand of the sea. They went up on the breadth of the earth and surrounded the camp of the saints and the beloved city. And fire came down from God out of heaven and devoured them."* Revelations 20:7-9

As mentioned in my earlier chapter that spoke about the Battle of

Armageddon the very nations that God uses to punish His people He will turn against and destroy after His people repent and cry out to Him.

Deception Warning Layer 3 - The Lie Personified, the Man of Perdition

To complete the sifting and make manifest those who are His against those who are not, another wave of deception will arise. This time every last soul that is not of God will be deceived. Even the very elect of God would be deceived if only such a thing was possible, but it is not possible to deceive God's elect. Paul speaking to the Thessalonians about the deception of these times said that God Himself will send a strong delusion so that all who do not love the truth will believe "the lie" 2 Thessalonians 2:9-12.

Jesus, here in this section of His schedule of events, gave us some clues that will do us well to heed. Matthew 24:26 *"So if anyone tells you, 'There he is, out in the desert,' do not go out; or, 'Here he is, in the inner rooms,' do not believe it..."* Finally a man who all, except God's elect, will believe to be Jesus Himself, will be going from place to place with masses gathering to him. It is possible that to fake omnipresence he will use holographic technology or look-alikes to give the impression he is omnipresent (is able to be present at multiple venues all at the same time.)

Chapter 8

The Great Deception
666 and the Mark of the Beast

Taunton Deane's MP Jeremy Browne said it had been a "horrendous accident".
He said: "There has not been a crash on this scale for many years and the implications of it will be life-changing for many people."
Eyewitnesses describe flames more than 20ft high and the sound of several crashes as the incident happened... [1]

It was thought that poor visibility from fog or smoke from a nearby fireworks display caused this horrific pile up of vehicles and the death of many.

Like this M5 crash in the UK, poor Spiritual vision is about to cause a pile up of crashes the sound of which will haunt our very souls. The sound of each crash will signify the eternal end of another person as they unsuspectingly plough into the trap of death and damnation. We warned but no one listened, each being too in love with the comforts and conveniences of today's modern Godless system.

---

[1] http://www.bbc.co.uk/news/uk-england-somerset-15603124 M5 Crash - 5 November 2011

The man behind the mark

Paul says he is the man destined for destruction but John labels him the antichrist the title that most are acquainted with. This man really will be the devil incarnate. Jesus came and lived among us as a man and the devil will try to do the same.

Jesus was born of Mary as a human baby, the devil also, though we are not too sure how, will at some point become a man. Isaiah and Ezekiel speaks of him as a man. Most agree that the king of Babylon spoken of in Isaiah is the devil. Isaiah prophesying about this king said, *"Those who see you stare at you, they ponder your fate: 'Is this **the man** who shook the earth and made kingdoms tremble, **the man** who made the world a wilderness, who overthrew its cities and would not let his captives go home?'"* Isaiah 14:16-17

Ezekiel again speaking of the devil but this time calling him the king of Tyre said, *"In the pride of your heart you say, 'I am a god; I sit on the throne of a god in the heart of the seas.' **But you are a mere mortal** and not a god, though you think you are as wise as a god."* Ezekiel 28:2

Daniel refers to him as the king of the north. See Daniel 11.

This will happen when satan becomes earthbound. Revelation records a battle in heaven where he will be defeated and thrown out. *"And war broke out in heaven: Michael and his angels fought with the dragon; and the dragon and his angels fought, but they did not prevail, nor was a place found for them in heaven any longer. So the great dragon was cast out, that serpent of old, called the Devil and Satan, who deceives the whole world; he was cast to the earth, and his angels were cast out with him.*

Then I heard a loud voice saying in heaven, 'Now salvation, and strength, and the kingdom of our God, and the power of His Christ have come, for the accuser of our brethren, who accused them before our God day and night, has been cast down. And they overcame him by the blood of the Lamb and by the word of their testimony, and they did not love their lives to the death. Therefore rejoice, O heavens, and you who dwell in them! Woe to the inhabitants of the earth and the sea! For the devil has come down to you, having great wrath, because he knows that he has a short time.'" Revelation 12:7-12

If we think we are having trouble now, wait until when the devil is thrown out of heaven and becomes a man. Many will say "But he was thrown out before the Genesis account". No, he had access to the earth but also still had access into heaven. We know from the Job incident that he had access into both heaven and Earth during the days of Job (read Job 1:6-7). In Luke 10 Jesus saw him fall from heaven. Revelation 12 said he accused the brethren day and night before God. There were no brethren pre-Genesis so this must be post Genesis and during the Church age as the term 'brethren' is New Testament language.

At the writing of this book the devil may still have access into heaven as he does earth but a time is coming when he will not. The devil in flesh, we know, will be a man who will exalt himself above even God. The Scriptures say he *"... opposes and exalts himself above all that is called God or that is worshiped, so that he sits as God in the temple of God, showing himself that he is God."* 2 Thessalonians 2:4 He will bring persecution against God's people as never seen before. He will rise as a man of peace but soon after show his true colours as a man of war. He is the beast of revelations, the head of mystery Babylon whom Jesus will destroy with the brightness of his coming.

Jesus had a forerunner in the form of John the Baptist and the antichrist too will have a forerunner known in scripture as the 'false prophet'. As seen in the Matthew 24:24, this man, the devil in flesh, the lie personified will come with the working of mighty false miracles to deceive. The miracle working false prophet will endorse the antichrist using his mighty false miracles to lead people into the devils death trap. Do not waste your time and energy or, for some of us, give away your cover (as true worshipers would have gone underground) to go see these men. True miracles point to God but lying signs and wonders will point to the antichrist and so persuasive will they be that even the elect will be tempted to think the antichrist is actually the Christ, but they will not fall for it. We do not need such issues to be struggling with at a time when we need to be focusing on the true Christ. When Jesus comes we all will know. Understand that in those days we will not need to go look for Jesus in some physical location because His arrival will come to us as lightning from the skies can be seen by all.

It was while on holidays in a Third World country that I realised how tightly bound we in First World countries are by our dependence on money. It's like satan is the spider, money his web and we the unsuspecting flies. In the more rural parts where we were staying, as we went on walks and moved about, we were picking and eating fruits that were larger, of better quality and taste than what we have to pay much money for in the supermarkets of a First World country. At one time we saw many ripe fruits on the ground under a particular tree, we thought they weren't edible. In our First World mentality we thought surely these can't be edible and just left there. We discovered that they were plums, some of the most juicy, tasty plums we have ever seen or tasted. Grapes were everywhere. We were walking up a road one day when we saw something looking like grapes hanging off the branches of a tree. We contemplated for a minute trying to work out what fruit grew on a tree but looked like grapes. Our investigation revealed that it was indeed grapes but it's vine had climbed and become one with this tree. We could pick and eat freely. I had forgotten how stress free life could be. God designed these things to be freely available but greed have restricted everything and made them only available to those who have money.

As it is in the First World today so shall it be throughout the whole world where nothing will be free. The few elites will control all the natural resources forcing everyone else to hand over their money in exchange for measly rations in tins and plastic packages. Scarcity is spreading like a blanket across the world through wars and the economic manipulation of the rich as they bring about a new world order where the masses are enslaved and controlled through finances. The black horse of Revelation 6 is already on his way. *"Then I heard what sounded like a voice among the four living creatures, saying, 'Two pounds of wheat for a day's wages, and six pounds of barley for a day's wages...'"* If you have lived in or even just visited a First World country for long enough you would have realised that money has become the source of life. We have been forced into financial dependency where today we can hardly do, have or be anything without money. This is just the precursor to the creation of the single global currency popularly known as the 666. As a nation's money bears an image of someone significant to that nation so the 666 will be the mark of the antichrist. The world's money will be 'the mark of the beast' and will confirm that those branded with it are owned by him.

"He was granted power to give breath to the image of the beast, that the image of the beast should both speak and cause as many as would not worship the image of the beast to be killed. He causes all, both small and great, rich and poor, free and slave, to receive a mark on their right hand or on their foreheads, and that no one may buy or sell except one who has the mark or the name of the beast, or the number of his name.

Here is wisdom. Let him who has understanding calculate the number of the beast, for it is the number of a man: His number is 666." Revelations 13:11-18 The idea here is that there will be no other option aside from the mark, nothing else in the world will be considered legal tender hence compelling everyone to take it. The problem is, taking the mark willingly or grudgingly doesn't make a difference. Once you are marked you have pledged your allegiance to him and have declared yourself the enemy of God.

It is Here

An article in the Financial Post carried the following heading...

> **"In Sweden, cash is almost extinct and people implant microchips in their hands to pay for things.**
> More than 4,000 Swedes have gone the microchip route as cash use fades and the government scrambles to figure out the effects on society and the economy."

Here is a snippet from the article.

> "Ask most people in Sweden how often they pay with cash and the answer is 'almost never.' A fifth of Swedes, in a country of 10 million people, do not use automated teller machines anymore. More than 4,000 Swedes have implanted microchips in their hands, allowing them to pay for rail travel and food, or enter keyless offices, with a wave. Restaurants, buses, parking lots and even pay toilets depend on clicks rather than cash."[1]

The global trends, pressures and technology are already in place ready for the man to step in and bring it all together.

---

[1] https://business.financialpost.com/news/economy/swedens-push-to-get-rid-of-cash-has-some-saying-not-so-fast
The New York Times, Liz Alderman, November 23, 2018, 6:30 AM EST.

Conclusion

The deception is now complete, layer upon layer. The false Church also called Mystery Babylon is now established with its central leader dubbed 'the king of Babylon' by Isaiah. At the very base of this Tower of Babel like structure are the false Christians giving heed to lying spirits and doctrines of devils that are preached by false apostles, prophets and pastors. They preach a false gospel that offers a false salvation and the receiving of a false spirit. At the top of this pyramid type structure will be the false Christ who will receive worship as a god. This is the man that will lead the effort to rid the earth of God's elect, both Jew and Gentile. It will be a repeat of what happened to Jesus when He was physically here. The only difference is that it will now be against the body of Christ worldwide and not just one individual. As Caiaphas led the effort to get rid of Jesus so this man will try to rid the earth of God's elect.

At the time of the writing of this book we were very conscious of the fact that he could appear at any moment.

Chapter 9

Earth's Desolation
After the Abomination

Based on Matthew 24:30-31

There will be great trouble for God's people but God will intercept that to bring trouble of His own.

The day of the Lord
The abomination has now been committed and those responsible have unleashed their hatred upon God's people not realising that God will answer with a desolation that will wipe out every living thing on the earth. The onslaught of man's terror will therefore be brought to an end by the return of Jesus for His elect and the beginning of the rain of God's terror upon the wicked. God is about to bring the destruction of the earth by fire. God will fight against those who fought against His people – Genesis 12:3, Zechariah 14:3, Psalm 35:1. But He must first remove His elect.

Matthew 24:30 The sign of the Son of Man
"Then will appear the sign of the Son of Man in heaven. And then all the peoples of the earth will mourn when they see the Son of Man coming on

the clouds of heaven, with power and great glory."

It would seem that all the peoples of the earth will first see the sign then an actual far away glimpse of the coming of our Lord with power and great glory. The peoples of the earth will not get a close up view as they could not stand to steer into His glory, yet even this glimpse will so terrify them that the whole earth will mourn. I figure the mourning will be by the ungodly as the elect, what's left of us, would now be rejoicing with joy inexpressible and full of glory as this would mark their deliverance from extreme persecution and the coming of the one they love so dearly and have waited for so expectantly.

Jesus says His coming will be as visible as lightning flashing in the east is visible even in the west. This could mean that the manifestation of 'His great glory' includes a marvellous display of heavenly lights that will be visible for all to see from one corner of the earth to the other. As John wrote in Revelation 1, this display could include the light from His eyes that were like blazing fire or the light from the reflections off His feet that were like bronze glowing in a furnace or the blinding light that came from His face that was like the sun shining in all its brilliance.

How long the sign of His coming will be evident in the sky we do not know, but one thing is sure, with the technology that we have today those who were not able to be outside to see it will most certainly pick it up on network television. *"..all the peoples of the earth... see the Son of Man coming on the clouds of heaven."* John in Revelation 1:7 repeats what Jesus stated here confirming that every eye shall see Him coming in the clouds and that all the peoples of the earth will mourn. Who wouldn't mourn at the sight of their imminent and inevitable death. Can you imagine the terror of those who realised they would go down with the Titanic into the deep, dark icy oceans with no hope of salvation. They persecuted and killed His people. They resisted and opposed everything He stood for and everyone who stood for Him and now they realise that He is real and is indeed the King of all glory.

Note that this is only the first phase of Jesus' return. Jesus' return will be in two phases, in the first phase He will gather His people but will only be seen in the clouds by the rest of the earth then He will actually arrive on earth with His people who were gathered to Him in the air (see Jude 1:14). This is not two comings! What I describe as the first phase is when we meet Him in the air on His way to earth, the second is when He actually arrives on earth. The gathering to Him in the clouds will take place at the sounding of the heavenly trumpet.

Matthew 24:31 The trumpet call
"And he will send his angels with a loud trumpet call, and they will gather his elect from the four winds, from one end of the heavens to the other."

Paul also speaks about things that will happen at the trumpet call in 1 Corinthians 15:52 and 1 Thessalonians 4:15-17. Jesus in Matthew 24:31 says the angels will gather His elect from the four winds and Paul speaking about this very moment shed some more light on some of the things that will happen during the gathering of God's elect. Paul says, *"For the trumpet will sound, the dead will be raised imperishable, and we will be changed."* 1 Corinthians 15 Not only will those that were dead be changed but we too who are alive at the sounding of this trumpet. He explains that, *"..the dead in Christ will rise first. After that we who are alive and are left will be caught up together with them in the clouds to meet the Lord in the air."* 1 Thessalonians 4 This, obviously again confirming that the sign of His coming in the clouds is a different event from His actual arrival on earth.

The angels will gather us. The dead in Christ will rise first then the living will join them and be taken to the Lord in the clouds in the air. During this process we will be clothed in the likeness of Christ by putting on immortality. John the beloved confirms this in his letter *"...we know that when Christ appears, we shall be like him, for we shall see him as he is."* 1 John 3:2b When we meet Him in the clouds we will behold the fullness of His glory. This we could not do in mortal flesh hence another reason why we must be changed. He will eventually come down to the earth when, with His feet, He will literally stand on the Mount of Olives.

Jesus' narration of events stops here but we have follow-up accounts from people like Peter, Joel and Zephaniah among others. It will be hell on earth after the angels have gathered the elect. *"...The heavens will disappear with a roar; the elements will be destroyed by fire, and the earth and everything done in it will be laid bare... That day will bring about the destruction of the heavens by fire, and the elements will melt in the heat."* 1 Peter 3:10 Knowing all this is about to happen what should we be doing? We should be living pure and godly lives as we diligently watch and wait.

"I will utterly consume all things from off the face of the ground, saith Jehovah. I will consume man and beast; I will consume the birds of the heavens, and the fishes of the sea, and the stumbling blocks with the wicked; and I will cut off man from off the face of the ground, saith Jehovah... The great day of Jehovah is near, it is near and hasteth greatly, even the voice of the day of Jehovah; the mighty man crieth there bitterly. That day is a day of wrath, a day of trouble and distress, a day of wasteness and desolation, a day of darkness and gloominess, a day of clouds and thick darkness, a day of the trumpet and alarm, against the fortified cities, and against the high battlements. And I will bring distress upon men, that they shall walk like blind men, because they have sinned against Jehovah; and their blood shall be poured out as dust, and their

flesh as dung. Neither their silver nor their gold shall be able to deliver them in the day of Jehovah's wrath; but the whole land shall be devoured by the fire of his jealousy: for he will make an end, yea, a terrible end, of all them that dwell in the land." Zephaniah 1:1-18

Chapter 10

Heed the Warning

Based on Matthew 24:32-51 and all of Matthew 25

Can you imagine the horrific screams Noah and the others in the ark had to endure that first night the ark was raised by the floods? Imagine the banging against its side that would start strong and rapid but soon fade into a deathly silence. The scraping sound of men and women digging their nails into its wood. Their nails getting ripped clean off their blooded fingers as they desperately clammer to get up the sides of the ark. As Noah endured those chilling calls for help no doubt he must have considered opening the door and letting some in. The problem however, was that it was God Himself who shut the door. What God has shut no man can open. The hell he had to endure that night, as he listened to death claiming its victims one after the other must have haunted Noah for the rest of his life. It is believed he warned his generation for about a hundred and twenty years but no one took heed.

The day of the Lord will be even more terrifying. *"And the kings of the earth, the great men, the rich men, the commanders, the mighty men, every slave and every free man, hid themselves in the caves and in the rocks of the mountains, and said to the mountains and rocks, 'Fall on us and hide us from the face of Him who sits on the throne and from the wrath of the Lamb! For the great day of His wrath has come, and who is able to stand?'"* Revelation 6:15-17

Matthew 24:32-35 Discern the Times
"Now learn this lesson from the fig-tree: as soon as its twigs become tender and its leaves come out, you know that summer is near. Even so, when you see all these things, you know that it is near, right at the door. Truly I tell you, this generation will certainly not pass away until all these things have happened. Heaven and earth will pass away, but my words will never pass away."

In the days of Noah the completion of the Ark was a clear sign that the pending destruction was close. Likewise we too, though we know not the day or the hour can have an idea how close the end is by what we observe. In Noah's day the first few drops of rain were forerunners heralding the coming flood.

In 1 Thessalonians 5:1-11 Paul explains that this day should not come upon us like a thief and this is exactly what Jesus' warnings are trying to do, to prevent us from being caught unawares. Jesus' second coming will surprise those who are drunk or asleep in the darkness of their souls. They cannot see at all, because they are asleep or they cannot see clearly because they are drunk and all this compounded by the fact that they are in darkness. On the contrary we are wide awake and watching, plus, it is bright all around us with the light of Christ like a sunny day, so we can see clearly and far. It will not surprise us. Awake oh sleeper, rise from your drunken state for the return of Christ is at hand. Are you watching, can you see it coming? To put it in simple terms, the vigilant watchman can see it coming but the sleeper is clueless. Proverbs 22:3 says this, *"The prudent see danger and take refuge, but the simple keep going and pay the penalty."*

Jesus says we are to watch and pray but what are we looking out for? We are looking for signs. *"He said to the crowd: 'When you see a cloud rising in the west, immediately you say, 'It's going to rain,' and it does. And when the south wind blows, you say, 'It's going to be hot,' and it is. Hypocrites! You know how to interpret the appearance of the earth and the sky. How is it that you don't know how to interpret this present time?"* (Luke 12:54-56) Need I say more? Can we not interpret the signs of this present time we are living in?

Matthew 24:36-51 No One Knows

Here Jesus steps away from giving a ball by ball account of the events to give us a warning. What is the warning? "...keep watch, because you do not know on what day your Lord will come." Jesus builds on the warning by giving an example from the days of Noah. "As it was in the days of Noah, so it will be at the coming of the Son of Man." Remember that the emphasis here is not on the lifestyle people will be living at His return but the fact that no one knows (see the start of vs. 36). Since none of us know when a fire may break out in our house let us see to it that our fire alarm is fit and working by constantly checking it and seeing to it that the battery has not run out. Since none of us know exactly when Jesus will return let us see to it that we are always ready and watching. If a fire breaks out and our fire alarm is not working we could be scorched to death. If Jesus returns and we are caught unawares and is not ready and prepared to meet Him we will be scorched to death.

The picture here is that of a watchman, if he falls asleep a whole city could be doomed but if he stays awake a whole city could be saved.

We must be ready when Jesus comes. Three times during His account of the end Jesus warns about deception and three times He told us to watch. In Matthew 24:4 He says *"Watch out..."* in verse 42 He says *"...keep watch"* and again in Matthew 25:13 He says *"...keep watch"* But how does one watch and get ready for the coming of Jesus? We should watch prayerfully as much of what is happening must be spiritually discerned. *"Watch therefore, and pray always that you may be counted worthy to escape all these things that will come to pass, and to stand before the Son of Man."* (Luke 21:36) Obey scriptures and live lives pleasing to God.

Another thing about the watchful person is that they are very conscious of their duties. Always in their minds is the fact that the master must be pleased at His return. Jesus gave an example in the parable of the faithful and wise servant Matthew 24:45-51. Those who have been charged to feed God's people must have done and still be doing so when Jesus returns. If we do not maintain a sense of His imminent return but begin to slack off in our minds and attitudes towards our master's house then we are going to be in deep trouble. Kindly note that this is not just for leaders but for everyone as we are all appointed to play a part in God's house, we are all a part of the body of Christ. Mark's account brings this out. He says in Mark 13:34-37 *"It's like a man going away: he leaves his house and puts his servants in charge, each with their assigned task,... What I say to you, I say to everyone: 'Watch!'"* Note that each servant has an assigned task.

Jesus has given us all the material we need to know from mere observation how close the end is. All we need to do now is take note of the things happening around us and remember what Jesus said. These pointers even came with warnings so woe unto us if we do not take head. Turn around, turn around, danger, danger, there is grave danger up ahead!

Matthew 25:1-13 The parable of the ten virgins
As we read through Matthew chapter 25 beginning with the parable of the ten virgins I would like to point out a few observations I made that could be easily missed by the casual reader. The first thing to note here is that all ten were virgins awaiting the bridegroom. They were all virgins, all waiting possibly, all beautiful etc. They were however, later separated into 2 groups based on nothing else except that of preparation. The prepared were branded as wise the unprepared as foolish.

Though it could be a general trait of the foolish virgins the truth is that Jesus only highlighted one area of oversight that separated the 2 groups. The foolish group had lamps but did not bring any oil to fuel those lamps. One wonders what was the point of the lamps if they had no oil. The only way I could make sense of their reasoning is to suppose that they thought it more likely that they would not need it as they would expect the bridegroom to arrive during the day. But Jesus said something that was key. He said *"The bridegroom was a long time in coming..."* Matthew 25:5 Due to the delay in the bridegrooms' arrival all got weary and fell asleep. Had they not fallen asleep they would have heard the coming of the bridegroom from afar off and run to get oil to prepare their lamps but their sleep made it a surprise.

"At midnight the cry rang out: "Here's the bridegroom! Come out to meet him!" Matthew 25:6 At this hour obviously one is going to need a lit lamp to find their way to the bridegroom so in a panic the foolish asked the wise for some of their oil. For this the wise said no because there might not be enough. We would have expected Jesus to rebuke these for being selfish and not sharing but instead He refers to them as wise. There are some things we have to do for ourselves, things that cannot

be shared with others even though they may be very close friends, our children or even a spouse. For one, we are all going to have to give account for ourselves before God, not for the other person.

If we share oil chances are there will not be enough for both of us. We would end up with say, 2 half full lamps when if I had kept my oil I would have a full lamp which would carry me twice the journey of a half full lamp. Not having enough to get to the bridegroom is a chance one cannot take. But then we could argue, "so why not travel together and share the light?" Maybe because different people walk at different paces and again this could cause a hold up. Whatever our arguments the obvious point is that getting to the bridegroom is an individual thing and cannot be shared like most other things having to do with Kingdom life.

Oil in the scriptures many times represents the Holy Spirit. We have the anointing of the Holy Spirit just as in olden days when one would be anointed with oil by a priest when chosen to do certain jobs. For example, David was anointed to be king by Samuel the priest. Today we are all kings and priest unto God and have been anointed by God with the Holy Spirit which represents the inauguration ceremony and an endowment of the ability to perform the job. The anointing of the Holy Spirit is an individual thing, this oil cannot be shared. To put it simple, the anointing cannot last if we got it from someone else. That feeling of the presence of God that we feel after a Sunday morning service will be gone by Monday morning. To get anointing that last we must pay the price, we must spend the time in the word and in prayer, we must value time spent with God. The pastor or the Church member who is always full of the Holy Spirit, peace and joy had to pay a price and you cannot get this same level of endowment simply by listening to or speaking with them.

Why midnight?
The fact that Jesus said the bridegroom arrived at midnight is no mistake or casual inclusion. As explained earlier when looking at Matthew 24:32-35 though we may not know the exact physical day and hour we who are watching do know the spiritual hour the Lord will return. Our Lord will return at the peak of spiritual night when the world is enveloped in spiritual darkness and the spiritual eyes of men are without light. John 1:4 says: *"In him was life, and that life was the light of all mankind."* Remember this scripture that was mentioned earlier? *"But first* [before his return] *he* [the Son of Man] *must suffer many things and be rejected by this generation."* Luke 17:25 The light of the world will be first rejected by the world before He returns. If the light is rejected the world will be left in thick darkness and dark it shall be at His return. Isaiah 60:2 puts it this way, *"See, darkness covers the earth and thick darkness is over the peoples,..."* Jesus will come at spiritual midnight but remember that only the spiritually discerning person can tell what spiritual hour it is.

The beautiful glow of lit cities all over the world can now be observed from as far as space. Never in our history has our nights been so well illuminated by man made light. As we overcome physical darkness we ourselves are being overcome by the darkness of our hearts and souls. We are presently slipping into the darkest of dark ages. If you wish to have an idea of what spiritual darkness looks like read Isaiah 59.

Matthew 25:14-28 The parable of the talents
Still on the topic of the end Jesus told His disciples this parable that had to do with investments. Again as with all His parables about the end Jesus made sure to speak not only of those who will gain but also of those who will lose out at His return. The loser in this case was the person who chose to bury his gold because they received only one talent. They did this because they were afraid to invest it but others

who had two and five talents were able to double their master's money. The one talented person had some things to say in his defence. He said the master was *"...a hard man, harvesting where you have not sown and gathering where you have not scattered seed."* This statement is either a desperate effort to find an excuse or an indication that he does not know his master. Our Lord is a compassionate, gracious, meek Lord and could never be described as a hard man.

Our master in turn described him as a wicked and lazy servant. Why are we wicked if we have no return on our talent to present to the Master when He returns? 1. Our talents or the gifts given to us like the gifts of the spiritual have been given to us for the edifying of the saints for the building of the body. These are to be invested for people and into people and where this does not happen lives are impacted. People need what God has given you, go see to it that they get it. 2. Trying to pass off our laziness as someone else's fault is wicked. This is a possible indication that Jesus will return in the midst of our present 'blame culture'.

Note: When Jesus returns He will be returning with something and He will be returning for something. He will be returning for His bride, His Church, a people that is without spot or wrinkle or any such thing. He in return, will come with rewards to distribute to us according to our performance while alive. What kind of reward will you be expecting? Jesus in Revelation 22:12 says, *"Look, I am coming soon! My reward is with me, and I will give to each person according to what they have done."* In Matthew 5:11 Jesus said, *"Blessed are you when people insult you, persecute you and falsely say all kinds of evil against you because of me. Rejoice and be glad, because great is your reward in heaven..."*

Matthew 25:31-46
The sheep and the goats

The return of Jesus will also indicate the time for judgement of the world. Here Jesus will separate from among the masses, those who are His and those who are not. Those who are His are described as sheep, those who are not, as goats. Some describe it as the great white throne judgement. Have you ever been to a prize giving before and watched the joys of others as they receive their prizes believing you deserve a prize but never heard your name called to receive one. In fact, some of us have been forced out of our jobs, victimised or just totally ignored after years of hard work, never receiving private or public appreciation, but that's ok. We should not seek the praises of men as we do the praises of our heavenly Father. The greatest feeling ever, will be the feeling one gets when told on that day to go to the right hand side of our Lord and to be presented with the prize of our heavenly inheritance. What will qualify us for such a great prize of eternal life? One answer is, the sacrifice Jesus made for our sins on the cross. The sign that we have received the seal of eternal life that Jesus purchased for us will be manifested in our kind treatment of Jesus directly while He was on earth or indirectly through His servants whom He now lives through.

Jesus is still alive in people and how we treat them bears a direct relation to the way we treat Jesus. Our unrepentant persecutors therefore stand no chance, and remember that there will be many in the last days. Be encouraged because what we see playing out here was also predicted by Paul in his second letter to the Thessalonians 1:5-6 *"...God is just: he will pay back trouble to those who trouble you..."* Vs. 41 of Matthew 25 indicates that a curse comes on those who do not consider God's people, how much more those who ill-treat them. They are marked for destruction on the day of the Lord. The curtains are drawn to close the penultimate scene of the programme with those on His left being led away to eternal punishment, but those on His right, the righteous ones, to eternal life. On which side will you be standing on that Day?

If you are presently not sure of your standing with God but desire to be on His right, I would strongly suggest that you repent now and turn back to God.

"See that you do not refuse Him who speaks. For if they did not escape who refused Him who spoke on earth, much more shall we not escape if we turn away from Him who speaks from heaven..." Hebrews 12:25

Thank you for reading. May the good Lord preserve us all spotless until the day of His coming.

Made in the USA
Columbia, SC
07 February 2022